FORGIVENESS

THE KEY TO FREEDOM

GERRI DI SOMMA

FORGIVENESS
THE KEY TO FREEDOM

GERRI DI SOMMA

forever
PUBLISHING LTD

FORGIVENESS, THE KEY TO FREEDOM

By: Gerri Di Somma

Compiled by: Lyn Birdsall

Published by: Forever Publishing

First Edition: December 2009

www.carmelcentre.org

Design and cover: www.cre8ion.co.uk

Printed by: J F Print Ltd., Sparkford, Somerset, UK

ISBN 978-0-9560549-5-1

All scripture verses are quoted from the New King James Version of the Bible, unless otherwise stated.

Abbreviations used: KJV - King James Version; NKJ - New King James Version

FORGIVENESS, THE KEY TO FREEDOM

CONTENTS

FORGIVENESS, THE KEY TO FREEDOM

PREFACE

God wants everyone to achieve their God-given potential and fulfil the destiny He planned and purposed for them. The Bible talks about us being living stones, individually formed and perfected by the master stonemason Himself, each for a particular place and function in the building of His kingdom. (*1 Peter 2:4-5.*) Also the Bible tells us that we are individually members of the body of Christ, the church, and it instructs us on the importance of functioning effectively where God has placed us with the responsibilities He has given us. (*1 Corinthians 12:27.*)

During many years of pastoring, counselling and teaching, I have encountered many stones which were crumbling, and I still find people like this now. Also, to use the other metaphor, there are members of the body who are clearly not in a condition to fulfil their part in it. These are people who have been hurt and emotionally bruised by others, by situations, or even by their own perceptions. They harbour bitterness and unforgiveness, which affects not just themselves, but many they are close to.

The bondage which unforgiveness brings is not only caused by failure to forgive others. Frequently it is the outcome of people not receiving God's forgiveness or not forgiving themselves. I strongly believe that people's understanding of forgiveness has been limited by lack of knowledge. All too frequently we hold the belief that forgiveness is merely ceasing to feel angry or bitter towards a person, but this is a small part of what the Bible teaches on forgiveness.

This book is based on biblical truth concerning forgiveness, unforgiveness and its consequences. As you receive a deeper understanding of these truths, God will empower you to implement them. Through His love, He has opened the way for you to be released from past hurts, bitterness and unforgiveness, to be set free and remain free from them.

As you read this book, allow God to speak to you and work in you through His Word. Allow Him to restore, re-shape and strengthen you. Let Him equip you to function to full capacity in your spiritual, emotional and physical life. Become one of God's 'living stones', become an effective member of the body of Christ, as you experience 'Forgiveness, the Key to Freedom'.

Gerri Di Somma

INTRODUCTION

WHAT JESUS SAID ABOUT FORGIVENESS

Jesus taught His disciples how to pray. On one occasion, He gave them a prayer which included in itself many aspects of prayer. It is often called 'the Lord's prayer'. *(Matthew 6:9-13.)* In it Jesus said we should begin, *"Our Father..."*, and should include asking the Father to *"forgive us our debts as we forgive our debtors."* Other translations refer to *debts* as *sins, trespasses* or *wrongs.*

Through His instruction to His disciples, Jesus tells us to seek forgiveness from our heavenly Father, but there is a condition. The condition is simply stated in the words, "*...as we forgive our debtors.*" We must be a forgiving people if we are to ask the Father's forgiveness for ourselves. When reciting the Lord's Prayer it's too easy to move on and set the challenge of forgiveness aside. Then we end the prayer with, "*Yours is the kingdom the power and the glory forever. Amen.*" We move on, but Jesus hadn't finished. He had more to say about forgiveness.

Jesus said: "*For if you forgive men their trespasses, your heavenly Father will also forgive you. But if you do not forgive men their trespasses, neither will your Father forgive your trespasses.*" *Matthew 6:14-15.* Jesus couldn't have made it clearer. The measure you apply will be measured back to you. God will only forgive to the degree that you are willing to forgive. If you want to remain secure in God's forgiving love, you must make sure that you keep your life completely clear of unforgiveness towards others, whatever the situation.

There is no such thing as justified unforgiveness. There is no act or sin that could be committed against you that is not forgivable, no matter how serious. Jesus' life demonstrated it and He taught it. If you want to be forgiven, then forgive.

We are all accountable to God

Jesus restated the necessity of forgiveness. He used a parable to explain certain principles concerning the kingdom and how they relate to the church. The parable begins: *"Therefore the kingdom of heaven is like a certain king who wanted to settle his accounts with his servants. And when he had begun to settle accounts, one was brought to him who owed him ten thousand talents. But as he was not able to pay, his master commanded that he be sold, with his wife and children and all that he had, and that payment be made." Matthew 18:23-25.*

As we read through the full parable we see that it reminds us that we are accountable to God for what we do with our lives. It shows us that as His servants we must conduct our lives at the same level that He does, particularly that His forgiving generosity must be expressed through us to the people we associate with. It also instructs us that to fail to forgive, whatever the situation, has serious consequences, that it imprisons us, can seriously affect others and ultimately can have eternal consequences.

We may not always be aware that unforgiveness is the root cause of various issues in our lives and that its damage to other people can be and may already have been widespread. However, Jesus recognised these dangers and kept His heart clear of unforgiveness. Jesus was man with the potential to sin, but He chose to live free from it.

The parable continues in *Matthew 18:26-31: "The servant therefore fell down before him, saying, 'Master, have patience with me, and I will pay you all.' Then the master of that servant was moved with compassion, released him and forgave him the debt. But that servant went out and found one of his fellow servants who owed him a hundred denarii; and he laid hands on him and took him by the throat, saying, 'Pay me what you owe.' So his fellow servant fell down at his feet and begged him, saying, 'Have patience with me, and I will pay you all.' And he would not, but went and threw him into prison till he should pay the debt. So when his fellow servants saw what had been done, they were very grieved, and came and told their master all that had been done."*

The servant had been forgiven and released by the master from an enormous debt. A fellow servant owed the servant but a pittance in comparison with his own previous debt to the master. Despite this, instead of extending his master's compassion to his fellow servant, he refused to forgive him.

Forgiving others is imperative if you want God to forgive you

As Jesus continued the story, He came to its central lesson: *"Then his master, after he had called him, said to him, 'You wicked servant! I forgave you all that debt because you begged me. Should you not also have had compassion on your fellow servant, just as I had pity on you?' And his master was angry, and delivered him to the torturers until he should pay all that was due to him."* And Jesus concluded the parable with a warning for us all: *"So My heavenly Father also will do to you if each of you, from his heart, does not forgive his brother his trespasses." Matthew 18:32-35.*

Through the parable, Jesus made the principle abundantly clear: we are to forgive as God has forgiven us. If we want to continue receiving His forgiveness, we must continually forgive others. If we do not forgive, there are serious consequences which are, in effect, like being in prison, something for which we are entirely responsible since God has enabled us to forgive through His compassion towards us.

Your life depends upon your heart remaining pure and free from unforgiveness. Even indulging your sinful nature for a moment could cost you everything you hold dear - your wife, your children, your friends, your neighbours - everybody. Jesus understood the destructive nature of unforgiveness and that's why He mentioned it so often.

Failure to forgive others hinders faith

Our faith cannot work if there is unforgiveness in our hearts. Unforgiveness is often expressed in bitterness, prejudice and negative attitudes towards others. If we fail to examine ourselves and deal with these issues, our faith will be severely hindered. This applies regardless of what may have happened historically or will happen in the future.

No one has ever been as wrongfully treated as Jesus was. He had more justification for holding others in unforgiveness than anyone has ever had. The very people He came to rescue, rejected Him, lied about Him and then eventually crucified Him. Yet there was no unforgiveness in Him which could hinder the miracles taking place through Him.

Have you ever wondered why we do not experience miracles, signs and wonders in the same way as Jesus? It could be that unforgiveness has barred the way. Deep in the recesses of our minds and hearts we often have some situation, some scar, which provokes our unforgiveness towards another. Though hidden, unforgiveness rarely fails to find a way of expressing itself through our words or actions. And by its nature it opposes and undermines the faith needed to see miracles in our day. The problem is not out there, it's not someone or something else; neither is there any cause to blame the devil, when the root problem is the sin of unforgiveness within our own hearts.

When I was preparing this, I too was challenged. I thought, "I'm the pastor. I should have overcome all this." I said to the Holy Spirit, "Examine me, test me now." The next minute I was in tears, pleading for Jesus to help me. I realised that if I had unforgiveness in my heart towards someone, I would be unable to help if God brought that person to me to ask for prayer for healing or anything else. Unless I dealt with my own unforgiveness, my faith for others would be affected.

Unforgiveness hinders prayer

On the subject of faith and prayer, we often quote Jesus' words from the following verses: *"Have faith in God. For assuredly, I say to you, whoever says to this mountain, 'Be removed and be cast into the sea,' and does not doubt in his heart, but believes that those things he says will be done, he will have whatever he says. Therefore I say to you, whatever things you ask when you pray, believe that you receive them, and you will have them." Mark 11:22-24.*

We frequently fail to read what follows. We stop there, becoming excited by such a great faith promise. But Jesus hadn't finished. *Verses 25-26* continue, *"**And** whenever you stand praying, if you have anything against anyone, forgive him, that your Father in heaven may also forgive you your trespasses. But if you do not forgive, neither will your Father in heaven forgive your trespasses."*

Jesus taught us that when we pray, if we have **anything** against **anyone**, we are to forgive them no matter what. If you don't forgive them, don't expect your heavenly Father to forgive you. Your prayers, however much you think you are praying in faith, will not be answered if you fail to forgive someone, no matter what the situation.

There is no limit to forgiveness

Thank God that Jesus' forgiveness knew no end and He freely went to the cross for us. We can be eternally grateful that our heavenly Father continues to forgive us when we confess our sin. However, His compassionate nature often finds little or limited expression in our lives.

Frequently we are something like Peter in our thinking: *"Lord, how often shall my brother sin against me, and I forgive him? Up to seven times?" Matthew 18:21.* Peter had grasped the principle that he must forgive and even thought he was being very generous. So Jesus' reply must have been quite a shock: *"I do not say to you, up to seven times, but up to seventy times seven." Matthew 18:22.* In other words, there is no limit to forgiveness. Don't even try to quantify it.

There are some believers today who consider seven a finite spiritual number which represents sufficient times for forgiveness to be applied. They look for some acknowledgement from God that they have done what is right and sufficient, that they have been generous enough. Many put a limit on the number of times they will forgive: enough and no more. Anyone who attempts to prescribe a limit on forgiveness, however they may express it, has failed to understand the nature of God and that forgiveness is to be without limit.

This reminds me of an amusing incident that happened while I was living and serving in a church in South Africa. A group of people from rough backgrounds became born again believers. One of them, whose background was particularly wild, became an usher. We were all at an important crusade and people were arriving. After a while we heard a big commotion and when we rushed to the scene we saw a man stretched out on the grass.

We asked the usher what had happened. He replied, "What I did was biblical. That man slapped me on one cheek. I turned the other cheek and he slapped me again. The Bible doesn't say anything after that, so I flattened him."

That is not how Jesus expects us to respond! He taught that we should forgive up to seventy times seven times. In the course of a day it would be like receiving a slap nearly every three minutes, then turning the other cheek and forgiving every time. We may think we are doing well when we forgive, but when we see it as Jesus said it, we realise there are insufficient hours in a day for all the forgiveness that God wants us to give. If people keep coming back and asking for forgiveness for what they've done to us, we must continue to forgive.

Love your enemies

The conversation with Jesus about forgiveness began when Peter asked Him how often he should forgive a brother who sins against him. Jesus' reply was therefore in the context of brothers in Christ. But this does not excuse us from forgiving those who are outside of that relationship, or those we may even consider to be enemies. Jesus did not make an escape clause for us anywhere. That is why we must purify our hearts, because God expects the same level of forgiveness towards everybody. Whether those who sin against us are in the church or outside, the same principle of love and forgiveness applies to all.

Jesus confirmed this, exhorting us: *"Love your enemies, do good and lend, hoping for nothing in return: and your reward will be great, and you will be sons of the Most High. For He is kind to the unthankful and evil. Therefore be merciful, just as your Father also is merciful." Luke 6:35-36.* For most people, it is easy to love family and friends, but here Jesus tells us that our love should go beyond these relationships. That is God's standard and Jesus was the perfect example of that standard. He was incredibly kind and merciful to the unthankful and evil, to those who hated Him, shook their fists and shouted at Him. Through this Jesus says to us that He wants us to show this same mercy to those who mistreat us, because forgiveness is an inherent aspect of His love.

Unforgiveness can have eternal consequences

Jesus continued: *"Judge not, and you shall not be judged. Condemn not, and you shall not be condemned. Forgive, and you will be forgiven. Give, and it will be given to you: good measure, pressed down, shaken together, and running over will be put into your bosom. For with the same measure that you use, it will be measured back to you." Luke 6:37-38.*

In this life, what we do and say generates a response from other people which reflects what we've said or done, whether good or evil. If we judge and criticise others, we should not be surprised if others do the same to us. However, this principle also applies in eternal terms in that God's response to us will reflect how we have conducted ourselves in this life with regard to others. If we have judged others, and not repented of it towards God, we carry with us into eternity something which cannot help but receive the judgment of God. *(Matthew 6:14-15; 18:35.)*

Thankfully, God has opened the way for us to repent, ask His forgiveness and counteract the negative seed we have sown by sowing the positive. None of us are exempt from the temptation to react negatively with people when they overlook, insult, bypass or treat us unpleasantly. All of us at some time have held on to unforgiveness and judgment, if only briefly. There may, even now, be unforgiveness in you, whether you realise it or not. There also remains the possibility you could fail to forgive at any time in the future.

When you consider this in the knowledge that God will hold you accountable for the way you treat others, it emphasises the importance of heeding everything that Jesus said about forgiveness and unforgiveness. Don't jeopardise your faith, your prayers, your relationships or your eternal destiny with God by holding unforgiveness in your heart. Forgive without limit and you will experience the same measure of God's limitless forgiveness towards you.

Knowing we should forgive, and why, does not tell us how to forgive. We now need to understand and recognise the causes and nature of unforgiveness, how to overcome it and how to avoid it if we are to enter fully the freedom our Father has purposed for our lives.

PART ONE
THE PROCESS OF UNFORGIVENESS

CHAPTER ONE

UNFORGIVENESS, THE DEVIL'S OPPORTUNITY

Our responses to present situations are determined by our past experiences. Because of this, our perceptions of what is happening in the present can be distorted by past hurts, causing us to measure every situation in the present based upon those past experiences.

This can be so powerful that there are times when we may be unable to respond normally to current situations and we react badly to them, sometimes even reacting violently to simple problems. When this happens it is a clear indication that we are emotionally bruised, bound by hurts from the past which make it very hard or impossible for us to live successfully. This is not God's desire or His purpose for us.

God's purpose is fullness of life

God wants us completely unhindered by any experiences that prevent us from leading a fulfilled and abundant life, one which demonstrates His presence and glory in every respect. One reason Jesus gave for His anointing and coming among us was: "*To set at liberty them that are bruised.*" *Luke 4:18 KJV.* When we recognise just how damaging emotional bruising is, it helps us understand God's heart in wanting us set free.

Dictionaries define 'bruise' this way: 'to injure without breaking the skin, to offend or injure somebody's feelings, not to be considerate, not to consider someone, to crush by pounding.' When we are hurt, usually no-one can see from our outward appearance that there is any problem. But inwardly it is a different story.

When our emotions are bruised, it offers the devil opportunity to bring his oppression and other devices into our lives and deny us the liberty for which Jesus died.

Satan's purpose is to bruise to establish opportunity

The 'bruising' of man is nothing new. God referred to it right in the beginning of the Bible. The devil had taken on the form of a serpent and had deceived Eve in the Garden of Eden. Following this, God spoke to the devil and foretold that he would bruise the heel of the Saviour to come. *(Genesis 3:15.)* What we need to understand from this is that bruising was Satan's purpose and method in order to steal, kill and destroy. But we also know that Jesus came to destroy the works of the devil. *(1 John 3:8.)*

Let me illustrate the issue we are confronted with. Often if you damage a piece of fruit a bruise appears. This begins a rapid process of decay which in most fruits makes it become bitter. What happens in people is that when, through some hurt, they become emotionally bruised, that bruising becomes a deep bitterness in their hearts. If they fail to deal with the hurt and bruising by seeking God, bitterness is the inevitable result, and this bitterness manifests itself in unforgiveness towards the source of the hurt. What is even worse is that living with bitterness can become a way of life for some people. Also, if the door is not firmly shut, Satan will walk in and claim squatter's rights to your life with which to destroy you and those you associate with.

It is vitally important to understand that, however painful it may be, it is not the hurt or the bruising which actually damage us. The destruction comes if we hold on to hurt feelings and let bitterness arise in us instead of applying reason based on the truth of God's Word, rather than our feelings. Letting hurt feelings remain unchecked leads to bitterness, the poison of the soul. It is this bitterness which has the potential to lead to our destruction.

Innocent children are Satan's prime target

Once we recognise that the purpose of Satan is to bruise and that he tries to cripple and bring down a person by bruising, we need to examine other tactics he uses. Please understand that I am not seeking to glorify Satan in this chapter, but to give understanding so we can walk in the freedom Christ bought through His blood.

Most of our hurt and bruising comes from things that happened when we were children. Adults have the capacity to evaluate situations in the light of their knowledge and understanding. They can apply the logic of reason to see clearly and not allow things which hurt and offend to damage their lives. They should be able to prevent what may have hurt and bruised them from affecting them.

Children, however, do not possess the same capabilities as adults. Children are largely innocent and vulnerable. Because of this they naturally place considerable trust and faith in adults. Hurtful things an adult says to a child may easily become accepted as truth. Then, because they are young, the bruising tends to be severe and becomes deeply embedded in their lives. Its effect becomes as if they've been cursed.

Satan aims to destroy the seed of woman

There are spiritual principles which affect every area of our lives. Once we recognise these principles, we can identify the spirit behind what is happening and begin to deal with each situation appropriately.

We have already recognised that Satan aims to bruise a person one way or another. What many of us may not realise is how Satan begins with innocent children in order to destroy the seed of woman. Sadly, throughout history to the present day, children's lives have been cut short in various ways, but it was and is not God's plan for this to happen to any child.

For example, the Bible recounts the story of Joseph, who was sold into captivity by his brothers when he was only a youth. His life could easily have been cut short. When we read about Moses, we discover that when he was only a baby, Pharaoh had ordered all Hebrew baby boys to be destroyed to stop their numbers increasing, and that would have included Moses if God had not intervened through the motherly instincts of Pharaoh's daughter. We later see history repeated when Herod attempted to destroy the infant Jesus' life by killing all children who were two and under in Bethlehem and the surrounding region.

The devil not only tries to destroy innocent children physically, but also emotionally. The weapons he commonly uses are fear and rejection, which are the primary causes of emotional destruction in a child. The potential effect can be devastating, and a rejected child can grow up finding it difficult or even impossible to love and receive love. A child who has been emotionally bruised may also express their hurt by withdrawing through fear, or, quite the opposite, through destructive and violent behaviour.

God's children are prime targets of Satan

New believers are also prime targets of Satan because of their new-found relationship with Jesus. As Jesus' enemy, Satan aims to sabotage the life of new believers who at first are like innocent children. They enter the church full of enthusiasm and want to get involved. They have been born again and they want to live their new life. If at this stage somebody says something that hurts and offends them, they may be unable to deal with it because of their relative spiritual immaturity and they easily become emotionally bruised.

The same principle applies to new ministries that are just becoming established, although Satan attacks God's children in every ministry.

His aim is to cripple them through misunderstanding and destroy them by lies and division. This is why it is so important to understand what is happening in the spiritual realm and deal with these issues according to the Word of God.

Unforgiveness opens the door for demonic influence

Unforgiveness can hold us in greater captivity by opening the door to the more sinister dimension of demonic influence, increasing our pain and torment.

To illustrate: consider a person who was sexually abused as a young child and was never able to work through the situation to forgive the one who abused them. What happens all too frequently as the child grows up and starts to develop sexually, is that the person experiences increased levels of lust in their life. This can drive them into things that can be very destructive for them and others.

The abused person may not be able to understand where all the lust has come from, and therefore not understand that behind it is an unclean spirit which came in on the back of the unforgiveness held against the one who abused them. That person gave the demonic spirit legal grounds to take hold of them through their unforgiveness, and mess with their life. They have become imprisoned through their unforgiveness and tormented by uncontrollable lust. Until they deal with the issue they have with the other person through forgiveness, they will not know the release they need in order to be free as God has purposed for them.

Another child who was physically or emotionally abused and has never forgiven the abuser, may grow up as a violent person. But once again, the demon comes in on the back of unforgiveness, deceiving and holding the person captive. He is now in the trap of the enemy's influence. This time, its fruit is in the shape of violence.

Jesus was bruised to fulfil God's purpose for us

God's remedy lies in His redemption of mankind. In *Genesis 3:15*

God also foretold the coming of Jesus. God said that although Satan may bruise Jesus, Jesus' victory over Satan would be complete, it would be a finished work. God declared to Satan: "*He shall bruise your head.*" Although the NKJV says 'bruise' in both instances in this verse, other translations say that Jesus will 'crush' Satan's head, which emphasises Jesus' victory.

Later on in the Bible, it is revealed that Jesus was indeed bruised. But it was not a victory for Satan; it was to fulfil God's purpose for us. *Isaiah 53:10* tells us that it pleased the Lord to bruise Him. It pleased God because it was the means to bring about His plans and purposes for mankind: *He was bruised for our iniquities. Isaiah 53:5.*

Satan tried to bruise the heel of Jesus to bring Him down in so many different ways. He was betrayed by Judas, a close friend, denied by Peter, falsely accused by the priests and hated by the crowd. Yet Jesus endured every situation, including what appeared to be His final destruction on the cross, with compassion for the lost. He took it all on Himself, so that we need not endure the consequences of the bruising the devil desires to inflict upon us.

Once we understand the price that Jesus paid for us and accept Him as our Saviour and Lord, we no longer need to endure the hurt of a betrayed friendship, of someone rejecting us, falsely accusing us or hating us. We no longer need to suffer hurt and bruising from anything or anyone whatsoever. Jesus has already carried that bruising on our behalf.

Understand Satan's intentions and use that knowledge to protect yourself from becoming a target. Even though Satan's purpose is to bruise and destroy God's children, rejoice in the good news that Jesus was bruised to fulfil God's infinitely better purpose for you and all who will accept Him.

CHAPTER TWO

CHANNELS OF HURT: CLOSE RELATIONSHIPS

There is enormous potential to become bruised through hurt arising in close relationships and relationships of trust. It's an area where we are particularly vulnerable and where we expect much and can be easily disappointed.

As we've seen, hurt leads to bruising and can easily end up in bitterness and unforgiveness. Where relationships are close and we are less on our guard, the opportunity to be hurt is never far away. It's not difficult to find families which have split apart because of this and some where individuals have no intention of being reconciled.

Parent and child relationships

Sometimes hurt comes from the relationship between parent and child. The following scripture shows us this: *A foolish son is a grief to his father, and bitterness to her who bore him. Proverbs 17:25.* Notice the reference to the mother's 'bitterness', her unforgiveness.

Ephesians 6:4 adds this: *And you, fathers, do not provoke your children to wrath, but bring them up in the training and admonition of the Lord.* The word 'wrath' includes resentment, bitterness and judgment in its meaning. In other words, Paul when writing to the Ephesians was saying: "You fathers, do not provoke your children to unforgiveness or bitterness, but bring them up in the training and admonition of the Lord."

Husband and wife relationships

Scripture tells us much about the relationship between a man and his wife. Here again we find bitterness and unforgiveness are concerns: *Husbands, love your wives and do not be bitter toward them. Colossians 3:19.* We would not be wrong in turning it around: wives, love your husbands and do not be bitter towards them. God warns both husband and wife to avoid bitterness because of its potential to damage and even destroy their covenant relationship of marriage.

Statistics reveal an alarming increase in the breakdown of marriage, resulting in separation and divorce. Although I obviously cannot know the reasons behind every broken marriage, my experience as a minister and counsellor has shown me that hurt is a major factor. The sad part about it all is that the hurt and bruising usually starts with something really simple or petty. They get entangled in their bruised emotions and the bruising turns to bitterness as emotions escalate out of control and separation appears to be the only solution to end the pain.

A simple example would be if a husband forgot his wife's birthday and she feels hurt because of it. This could be because she perceives it as a sign that he does not love her, or that it was his intention to hurt her. Either way, inwardly she is hurting, although she may not at first show it outwardly. She may even begin to joke about his forgetfulness. But as her jibes at him continue, he too becomes hurt. In this way the relationship goes from bad to worse, unfounded suspicions arise and suddenly become issues in themselves. Then both the husband and the wife become bitter towards each other, and…so it goes on.

Unfulfilled expectations are a seedbed of hurt

We must recognise that unfulfilled expectations can easily lead to hurt and bruising. This can often result in us blaming others for the condition of our lives, and then it's only a short step to bitterness and unforgiveness.

What is an unfulfilled expectation? We all have expectations in life; we expect certain things from people, for them to be or do something for us. When we perceive that person has or those people have failed to do what we expected, we are well on our way to feeling hurt and let down. The hurt then sits and ferments into a big bruise.

Perhaps we see ourselves as having been rejected, or we see someone as not having sufficient care and concern for us. Maybe we feel we have not been properly recognised and respected. Perhaps resentment crept in because you consider you've not been fairly treated: "And don't they know that because they have not done what they said they would do, I'm left with a lot of things to do which I shouldn't have to do!" You can add your examples from your own experience.

Sometimes we can end up measuring our lives and the resulting success or lack of it from the position of how we see others have failed us: "If they had only done this or that, life would have been quite different and I wouldn't have had to struggle like I have." We conclude that where we are today is because of the failure of others in what we perceive as their responsibility towards us.

You may say that you didn't have a great education; that your father never hugged you and your mother never told you that you were good-looking. You can come up with any number of things. You possibly feel that it's their fault that you are a mess. But if you could step out of your hurt you would see that, although what happened may be true, none of it was the real reason for the difficulties you now face. It is only when we allow those circumstances to affect our lives negatively through hurt and unforgiveness that our lives become a mess.

Many people struggle in this area, and it is particularly evident within father and child relationships. If a father never affirms or expresses his love for his child, whether boy or girl, that child grows up with unfulfilled expectations, feeling unloved and rejected. As a result, their sense of self-worth can become seriously affected through that failure to receive the father's approval. Throughout childhood, puberty and through to adulthood, the person who was hurt as a child continues to make decisions in life which are affected by that hurt. This will often result in the child blaming the father for their life's situation.

Unfulfilled expectations do not need to lead to bruising, bitterness and unforgiveness. We can break the pattern by appreciating that God gave each one of us this life, and understanding that we are responsible for how we live it. We can bring change by recognising that our parents were in fact stewards of God's property. You may never have considered this to be the case, but *Psalm 127:3* tells us: *Children are a heritage from the Lord, the fruit of the womb is a reward.* Even if our parents did not do a great job, we still have our mind, our intellect and the ability to make our own decisions. Therefore we have what it takes to make right choices and decide not to hold anything against our parents.

The first thing we need to do is to forgive and release those we have held in unforgiveness because of our unfulfilled expectations. How we do that, I will explain in detail later. We can greatly help ourselves in the first place by not having expectations of others. People do fail. We fail. Life's like that.

Take, for example, an elderly person who had unfulfilled expectations as a child. I have met some who still are yearning for approval from a father who died many years earlier. As children, we expect our parents to affirm us or to be told we are loved. But as we grow older and get a grip on life, there is no need to hurt ourselves through our expectations. Once we understand that God affirms us, loves us and tells us of His love for us, we no longer need another person's approval, because we know we have God's approval.

We need to stop striving for what we may never receive from someone, because there is nothing we can do about it, and the striving will just make the bruise bigger. We need to forget what happened in the past and forgive those who we feel have let us down.

The deepest hurts can arise in any close relationship

Those we care about the most have the potential to hurt us the most. Often our expectation is more subtle than an obvious demand. It may be an inference or expectation through perceived association. Some think they have a special relationship and expect more, particularly more recognition. It may even come from an expectation to do with a tradition or habit installed in our subconscious by others we have known which we have not consciously accepted, but has and does affect the way we perceive things all the same. But these deposits of expectation can so easily become the source of our hurts when relating to others.

If a stranger walked up to you in the street and said, "I hate you. I think you are the worst person in the whole world," it would undoubtedly shock you, but it probably would not have much long-term effect on you. But if your best friend said that to you, how would you feel then? I am sure you would be deeply hurt and the effect on you would last longer. This is because the greater the knowledge of the other person, the greater the degree of the hurt.

When the church which my wife and I started was very small, it was really easy to touch base with every person there. We knew every member and virtually everyone who attended the church in those early days. They came in and out of our house and we also visited them. But as the church began to grow and the invitations multiplied, it became increasingly difficult to do the things we did.

Another aspect of this was that every time we accepted an invitation, we were blessed, not just because of the fellowship, but because our hosts always prepared the best and most delicious food. This presented us with another practical challenge. We did not want to hurt or offend our hosts, but with so many invitations we really had to watch our food intake for the sake of our waistlines.

There was a more serious problem. As the church grew, some of the people who were with us in the early days weren't too happy about 'sharing' us with more people. They wanted our attention as they always had done. We became aware that, as a result, hurt was beginning to creep in, a kind of resentment and pain. Some people were hurt because I could no longer automatically do house visits as before. They felt they were being denied something by being required to invite us and wait until we could visit. To them our 'special relationship' was being eroded and they were being neglected.

The rationale of the situation was obvious, but some were not prepared to apply themselves to the changing circumstances, but preferred the hurt by which they justified their complaint. Some expected me to know about their need without them telling me, as if there was some pastoral magic which absolved them from any responsibility in the relationship. Then their hurt increased because they saw me visiting other people or heard indirectly that I had been to see someone they considered less deserving than them.

This is typical of how people respond in close relationships. We make assumptions and have expectations which are easily hurt if not fulfilled. When situations arise which could hurt us, we should not become upset and blame the other person. If we are hurt, we should recognise the problem is with us and not with them. It is all in the way we perceive things. These situations provide Satan with a prime opportunity to do his destructive work.

This does not have to be the way it is. Hurt has the capacity to hold us in bondage, but it need not end up in our destruction. In fact, hurt does not have to be our experience. Even so, we have already seen that God's purpose in Jesus being bruised was to fulfil His plans for us to live in His glorious freedom. This is the 'good news' referred to in *Luke 4:18,* where Jesus declared that He came *"to heal the brokenhearted, to proclaim liberty to the captives and recovery of sight to the blind, to set at liberty those who are oppressed (bruised, KJV)."* We also read Isaiah's prophetic words revealing to us that Jesus was *wounded for our transgressions and bruised for our iniquities.* The words that follow tell us that *the chastisement for our peace was upon Him, and by His stripes we are healed. Isaiah 53:5.*

Unforgiveness always results in broken relationships

It is very sad but true that unforgiveness, with all its bruised and bitter fruit, can cut people out of our lives. When someone hurts or disappoints, it is very likely that we will choose not to have contact with them any more, or no more than has to be. But even though you may not see them physically, they still remain part of your life emotionally. This is because, although contact may be severed, the emotional tie remains because of how we feel about them.

This has a cumulative effect. Whenever we encounter another situation in the future with someone else who brings back the memory of the original hurt, we will tend to cut that person out of our lives too. We live in fear of further pain, yet are unable to avoid it as our continued unforgiveness perpetuates one broken relationship after another.

Man was not created to live in isolation, to be self-sufficient. He was created first for fellowship with God and next for fellowship with others. The whole of Ephesians chapter four highlights the importance of these relationships. *Ephesians 4:3* exhorts us all *to keep the unity of the Spirit in the bond of peace.* As we read on, the Word instructs us how we can contribute to that unity and shows us the ways in which sin can cause disunity. God's plan and purpose for us is to live in harmonious relationship with others and for us to do whatever we can to maintain that harmony.

Unforgiveness towards man grieves the Holy Spirit

There are so many ways in which sin can break down our relationship with God. When we consider the work of the Holy Spirit in our lives in taking us forward in God's purposes for us, it is not difficult to see that our ungodly attitudes and responses, particularly unforgiveness, give Him grief.

This truth is expressed in *Ephesians 4:30-32: Do not grieve the Holy Spirit of God, by whom you were sealed for the day of redemption. Let all bitterness, wrath, anger, clamour, and evil speaking be put away from you, with all malice. And be kind to one another, tenderhearted, forgiving one another, even as God in Christ forgave you.*

God's love for us is so great that He sent His Son Jesus to die in our place, to take our sin upon His shoulders and forgive us our sins. It is a love so great that He gave His Holy Spirit as our Helper; a love so great that He longs for us to live in unity and peace with Him and others; a love so great that He provided His Word to teach and guide us in every situation and in every relationship.

As believers, we need to heed the exhortations given in Ephesians, apply the wisdom of the Word and let go of unforgiveness. The more human relationships are broken, the more the Holy Spirit is grieved and the more our relationship with God is affected.

Broken relationships cause insensitivity

Through unforgiveness we separate ourselves from God and others. As a result we have to control and determine what happens in our lives without God's help. We try to do this through our own wisdom and ability. Vainly we suppose that we can control and determine our destiny and everything else. In doing so we become insensitive to God and there is no room for Him because we act 'like' God. In this state of mind, we become the centre of our own universe and expect others to conform to our will and expectations. We become insensitive to others because we are so focused on ourselves.

We only have to read *James 3:14-18* to be reminded of how self-centred we become when we do things our own way and do not apply God's wisdom. As a result, our attitudes become insensitive and critical towards other people and we have no proper regard for their needs. *If you have bitter envy and self-seeking in your hearts, do not boast and lie against the truth. This wisdom does not descend from above, but is earthly, sensual, demonic. For where envy and self-seeking exist, confusion and every evil thing are there. But the wisdom that is from above is first pure, then peaceable, gentle, willing to yield, full of mercy and good fruits, without partiality and without hypocrisy. Now the fruit of righteousness is sown in peace by those who make peace.* If we are to tap into God's wisdom and let Christ be formed in us, we must eradicate unforgiveness.

Broken relationships result in spiritual and emotional immaturity

When hurt, bruising and bitterness have led to broken relationships and we have distanced ourselves from God, both our spiritual and emotional growth become stunted and result in immaturity. This is something that Paul was aware of and had to deal with in the church of Corinth: I, brethren, could not speak to you as to spiritual people but as to carnal, as to babes in Christ. *I fed you with milk and not with solid food; for until now you were not able to receive it, and even now you are still not able; for you are still carnal. For where there are envy, strife, and divisions among you, are you not carnal and behaving like mere men? 1 Corinthians 3:1-3.*

Paul's statement shows the relationship between the natural and the spiritual and how the one affects the other. Paul recognised spiritual immaturity in the church when he was faced with the evidence of bitterness in their attitudes and behaviour. He rebuked those concerned, telling them they were living carnally. He implored them to grow up and begin to live like adults who are spiritually mature.

The importance of maturing is confirmed in *1 Corinthians 13:11: When I was a child, I spoke as a child, I understood as a child, I thought as a child; but when I became a man, I put away childish things.* Paul's words remind us that we have a God-given responsibility to grow up, both spiritually and emotionally. This is not only for our sakes, but for the sake of others, as the early part of *1 Corinthians 13* makes clear.

One of the reasons that broken relationships cause immaturity is because emotional growth can stop at the time of the bruising. This immediately produces problems because we are then snared by our own immaturity.

Let us say that at the age of ten, something terrible happened to you. You became emotionally bruised and as a result a significant part of your emotions remained at that place of hurt. In the meantime, your life went on and you continued to develop and grow, physically and socially. It is out of such a background that we find fully grown people respond at times like ten-year-olds, because they have not forgiven and released the source of their hurt.

People in such a situation as this, whether they realise it or not, then make decisions in life which are adversely affected by the consequences of an encounter they had as a ten-year-old. When you understand this, you can see why many people make decisions which are so immature and self-centred.

To be spiritually and emotionally mature, there must be forgiveness and healing. When the healing comes, it must first be at that place where the initial hurt came as a ten-year-old. This immediately releases and restores you to the place where you can walk on in spiritual and emotional maturity. If there have been additional areas of hurt and unforgiveness as a result of that initial hurt, those must be dealt with immediately, and you must grow up.

You don't have to be hurt by the darts that are often thrown at you by what people say or do. But allowing a hurt to become a bruise which decays to bitterness and unforgiveness is inevitably going to damage you, and others. Guard your relationships with a heart of compassion. Be quick to forgive and move on in obedience to the Lord and fulfil His calling on your life.

CHAPTER THREE

IDENTIFYING BITTERNESS IN YOUR LIFE

You cannot overcome bitterness before you are able to recognise its existence in your life. Let us therefore take a look at some patterns of behaviour which are common among people when bitterness is within their heart.

Bitterness is linked to unforgiveness

The Bible exhorts us to *run with endurance the race that is set before us. Hebrews 12:1.* In order to do that, we are told we need to renew our spiritual life, to *lay aside every weight, and the sin which so easily ensnares us.* The writer then continues to outline various weights and sin that we need to deal with, and he includes 'bitterness'. *Hebrews 12:15* puts it this way: *Looking carefully, lest anyone fall short of the grace of God; lest any root of bitterness springing up cause trouble, and by this many become defiled.* The Amplified Bible refers to *a root of resentment, rancour, bitterness or hatred.* From this we can see that the word 'bitterness', from its extension used in the Amplified, connects with words associated with unforgiveness.

One source defines unforgiveness this way: 'to bear malice, cherish a grudge, nurse resentment, evil intent, hostility, spite; abusive and savage.' It has also been defined as: 'Not willing to forgive or excuse faults; harsh, hostile.'

Bitterness can be defined: 'Feeling angry, hurt, resentment; aggrieved, embittered, jaundiced, rancorous, resentful, sour; unwelcome to the mind, causing sorrow; showing or feeling caused by mental pain or resentment'.

These definitions indicate that bitterness and unforgiveness are really much the same thing. When you have a root of bitterness, it is because you have a root of unforgiveness in you.

Choosing not to forgive supposes that you can be like God

Few people realise the full destructive extent of unforgiveness. The reason it is so damaging is because when we choose not to forgive someone, we are, in effect, judging them as unworthy of being forgiven. The Bible tells us that we are not to judge anyone. To ignore this is to infer that we are in a position equal to or greater than God. We may not deliberately set out to do this, but to judge someone unworthy of our forgiveness is to make ourselves like God in our view of the other person, whereas God alone is the righteous Judge.

Bitterness comes out in our speech

The book of Job in the Old Testament describes human suffering at every level, revealing truth that applies to us today as well. It is a warning to us against becoming bitter towards God, particularly in the face of challenging circumstances which test our faith. The positive outcome that Job experienced after all his hardships should encourage us to trust God for our deliverance and restoration, no matter what happens to us.

Job learned his lesson the hard way. He was a wealthy, influential man who was righteous and who loved God. In those days, it was widely believed that prosperity was God's reward for goodness and that calamity was God's judgment because of the individual's sin. When calamity began to strike at every possible area of his own life, Job not only experienced emotional and physical suffering but was inwardly tortured, because he knew that he had done nothing to merit such 'judgment'.

As a result, bitterness towards God began to take root in Job's heart until he could not contain it. His bitterness spilled out in his speech and He began to question God and to complain against Him, declaring: *"I will not restrain my mouth; I will speak in the anguish of my spirit; I will complain in the bitterness of my soul." Job 7:11.*

Instead of checking and correcting his attitude, Job allowed his bitterness towards God to escalate. Eventually it reached the point where he claimed that he was right and God was wrong. In this embittered state, he sinned and rebelled against God. *(Job 34:4-6; 34:36-37.)* What came from his mouth polluted him and was destroying him.

Some people only have to open their mouths and their hurt is quickly revealed by what they say or the way they say it, as we see with Job. When I am counselling such people, they often make repeated references to one particular person or situation. Any such symptoms provide an immediate indication of a deeply-rooted problem involving unresolved hurt and bitterness within. I then know that all I need to do is to explore that area long enough and I will discover their real problem and what the relationship was in which their hurt originated.

Bitterness is seen in actions and behaviour

If you observe people long enough, you will recognise that it is not only their speech that reveals hurt within. People's actions and behaviour will also show you that there are challenges in their lives. In the following scripture, the apostle Paul highlights this, and begins with an exhortation: *Let all bitterness, wrath, anger, clamour, and evil speaking be put away from you, with all malice. Be kind to one another, tenderhearted, forgiving one another, even as God in Christ forgave you. Ephesians 4:31-32.* He lists a number of ways we can sin in regard to relationships, but he also presents the godly alternative, behaviour towards others which is motivated and achieved through a forgiving heart.

Here we see that all bitterness and unforgiveness is listed with wrath, anger, clamour, evil speaking and all malice. In fact, all of these can come out of a heart of unforgiveness. These can and often do become evident in our actions. For example, a sure sign of bitterness is when someone overreacts to the simplest or the silliest little thing. When we look to the root issue we find, almost without exception, that there's hurt and unforgiveness which have arisen from a relationship that went sour.

Relationships with our parents are often the source of so much of this. We get hurt when we think they don't affirm us as they should. When they are alive, we often try to manipulate them to meet our unmet needs. When they are dead, we often refer to them when reflecting on our hurts.

The troubled area of gender confusion

While on this subject of a child's need for affirmation, let me mention the importance of affirming a child's gender. This can have an enormous impact on them as they begin to develop an awareness of their sexuality. If their gender is not effectively affirmed, it can lead to gender confusion, which can be found all through our nation and worldwide. This is evident in the increasing deviation from God's plan and purpose for male and female relationships. Homosexual and lesbian relationships, and transvestite and cross-dressing behaviour, are now accepted by society as 'normal', and are increasing. By far the highest evidence is found in male to male relationships.

I believe one of the most significant reasons for this is because parents - fathers in particular - don't do what they are supposed to do. Fathers fail when they don't affirm their son's masculinity and when they do not affirm their love as a father for their son. They fail when they do not affirm their son as God did when He declared His love to Jesus: *"You are My beloved Son, in whom I am well pleased." Mark 1:11.*

These problems are compounded in today's society which endorses single parenting, because many children grow up not knowing their father. They live with their mother, who does a marvellous job of looking after them, but she is unable to provide the influence and example of a masculine role model that only a father can. Boys need a father to take them out, to climb trees, cook over a camp fire, and do exciting, challenging and even dangerous things (health and safety permitting). Doing 'boy things' with Dad is so important because of what it teaches the child in his development towards manhood. Boys who do not have a father's manly influence miss so much.

I strongly believe that boys and girls alike need the security and example of both parents to maintain a healthy emotional development. Every child needs to know that they are loved. They need the affirmation of both Mum and Dad. When this is not forthcoming, it not only results in gender confusion, but it opens a door for hurt and bitterness to walk in, not to mention give Satan a prime opportunity to do his destructive work.

Bitterness is revealed in attitudes

Bitterness is not only revealed through speech, actions and behaviour but also through our attitudes: *For as he thinks in his heart, so is he.... Proverbs 23:7.* It is a person's attitudes and how he thinks that shape his actions. For example, a recluse chooses that particular lifestyle not because he wants to live in isolation as such, but because of something in his life that causes him to shun humanity. Few of us may be able to understand the attitude of someone whose lifestyle differs so significantly from what we consider to be normal. We need to recognise the likely presence of deep-rooted bitterness and unforgiveness. It is this which has caused him to lose hope and faith in people and has affected his attitude towards life profoundly. God never created us to live life alone, but to interact with others for our mutual benefit. *"It is not good that man should be alone; I will make him a helper...." Genesis 2:18.*

Prejudice is another attitude which reveals hurt and bitterness and can affect other people on a large scale. My wife and I witnessed this first-hand because we grew up in South Africa in a climate of racial prejudice. The attitudes, actions and behaviour of those who were prejudiced resulted in innocent people being victimised, attacked and hated by those they had never harmed. Many of the victims in turn became hurt and embittered. Some of the victims retaliated with negative attitudes, actions and behaviour. There are many people, both black and white, whose attitudes towards others reveal that forgiveness and healing need to take place.

But other people responded differently, with a forgiving heart. It's a fact that two people may experience the same situation, the same victimisation and hatred from others, but respond in completely different ways. For example, in the Truth and Reconciliation Forums held in South Africa after the fall of the apartheid government, some people were able to forgive those who had committed the most heinous atrocities. Nelson Mandela was a prime example of someone who was able to express true forgiveness, but there were many others who remained, and still remain, unable to forgive.

We all need to examine our own attitudes, because they affect our relationships with others. If you have noticed that no-one wants your company, ask yourself, "What's coming out of my mouth? What kind of attitude do I have?" Perhaps you do not want the company of certain people because of the bitterness within you. But, if your bitterness continues, eventually you will be shunned by everybody, because nobody wants to be in the presence of people who speak words of bitterness every time they open their mouths.

Bitterness causes breakdown in physical health

Eventually bitterness always finds an expression or a route along which to reveal itself, and that can be through ill-health. We see this described in *Matthew 4:24: They brought to Him all sick people who were afflicted with various diseases and torments…and He healed them.* Their bodies were afflicted and their minds and emotions were afflicted as well.

The following real-life situation demonstrates this powerfully. I once knew a lady who was absolutely riddled with rheumatoid arthritis and was very bent and crippled, even though she was young. She believed in God, but she did not have a relationship with Him. Then, one day, she received Jesus Christ as her Lord and Saviour. Once she knew her heavenly Father through Jesus, her life began to change dramatically.

There had been a long history of emotional hurt in her life and verbal abuse from her father. When she became a Christian, she was empowered to go through the process of asking God to forgive her for her bitterness towards her father. She was then able to release him in her heart for the abuse and to ask God to forgive him.

This dear lady who had been ill for so long was not only emotionally restored but was also completely healed of her rheumatoid arthritis. All that remained were slight kinks in two fingers, the only indication that she once had rheumatoid arthritis. These painless 'scars' reminded her never to fall into the snare of bitterness and unforgiveness again, but to check her heart continually. She later became a lecturer in the Bible School where I taught and it was wonderful to see her serving God in a way that previously would have been impossible.

Numerous ailments that people experience have their root cause in bitterness. If we could look within the hearts of people suffering from ill-health, I am certain we would discover a root of bitterness in many.

God wants us whole in spirit, soul and body. This becomes possible when we trust completely in Jesus and take our eyes off people and circumstances that have hurt us: *You will keep him in perfect peace whose mind is stayed on You.' Isaiah 26:3.* When God's peace flows through us it keeps us content and healthy. When people are full of bitterness, they lack peace and they do not even sleep properly. Think of a time when you had an argument with somebody and you did not sort it out before bed time. It is quite probable that you did not sleep well that night.

God even warns us about that situation. The Bible says: *Do not let the sun go down on your wrath. Ephesians 4:26.* Do not let the sun go down on your judgment. Deal with it, pick up the phone. Your sleep may depend upon it. When bitterness affects sleep, it produces a vicious spiral. Without good sleep, an attitude that was wrong in the first place becomes worse; you become irritable and then you say and do things that cause you to fall into all kinds of unhelpful responses. Added to that, prolonged lack of sleep affects physical health.

Bitterness pollutes others

Even beyond the damage that bitterness causes the individual who is bitter, the real tragedy lies in the way that bitterness can pollute others. Through your own bitterness you can cause others to become bitter, twisted, resentful and unforgiving without a just cause. They do not even need to go through the experience that caused your bitterness, because you can train them in how to be bitter from your experience.

For example, imagine a young married couple, with a little girl of two years. The husband leaves his wife and daughter and runs away with another woman. The wife then tells the little girl, "Look what your father's done to us. Your father's a rat. All men are rats, I hate your father, I hate men, and they're just no good. You can never trust them."

Through the mother's unforgiveness and bitterness, that young girl grows up with the same impression of men that her mother has. She has not had the same experience as her mother, but she has taken on her mother's hurt, not to mention the hurt she herself may have felt. That bruising affects her, and as a result she reacts towards men in the same way as her mother does. The mother's bitterness has polluted the life of her daughter, and so the bitterness is perpetuated.

Whatever the situation, we need to understand the principle that hurt people hurt people. *Hebrews 12:15* tells us we should be on guard, *looking carefully lest anyone fall short of the grace of God; lest any root of bitterness springing up cause trouble, and by this many become defiled.* Through bitterness and unforgiveness, many become defiled or polluted. So when you carry hurt, you can affect people round about you, and you might not even be aware that you are doing it. You may hurt a little child, a family member, another believer, a friend or colleague. No matter who it may be, when you do not deal with your hurt and bitterness, it affects others.

This principle is re-stated in *1 Corinthians 15:33*, which says, *Evil company corrupts good habits.* Some translations say *good morals.* Hurt people do not heal people; hurt people hurt people. On the other hand, people who have been healed help others to be healed and made whole.

It is important to become aware of what impact your unresolved hurt will have on others. One place where you can see what is going on in relationships is within the church, which itself is an example of family life on a larger scale. If you watch someone who is disgruntled, you can see how they affect others. At first they will just influence a small group of people closest to them, and then it spreads to more and more people. Eventually, the one who is offended leaves the church and drags some of the others along too. Then those who go along with them become even more severely hurt because they are no longer in the safety and protection of where God had placed them.

Bitterness builds walls of separation

Building walls between yourself and others can indicate the presence of bitterness. This can happen in any sphere of life, and even within the church family.

In *Matthew 18* Jesus explained to His disciples the importance of forgiveness, using the context of church life. In *verses 15-20* He described a situation where a brother sins against another. He explained that there is a correct process to follow in order to restore the brother to God and the church. *Verses 19 and 20* tell us that the aim of this is also to restore unity in the church, because agreement brings God's answers and God is present when His people gather in His name. *Verse 21 and 22* tell us we should forgive indefinitely, even when a brother does not repent.

If, for example, someone in the church offends me on a serious matter, my reaction may be to tell other people. But that is not what Jesus instructed His disciples. My first response should be for me to approach that person and explain, face to face, how I feel. If what I say is accepted, the person will respect the fact that I have made personal contact to try and resolve the issue, and the result will be reconciliation.

If what I say is not accepted, I must then ask one or two others to help me and go with me as witnesses to the attempted reconciliation. If after that, the person is still full of bitterness and refuses to repent and be reconciled, then we must present the situation before the church.

I have tried and I am still trying to make right with him. I do not want a root of bitterness to be formed in my heart, but this is just what will happen if I don't go to him to seek resolution. I must give the other person the opportunity to explain from their perspective, thereby finding a basis for reconciliation. Going before the church is the last resort, after all other efforts have failed.

The reason for this biblical course is to bring witnesses to test my claim of a wrongdoing towards me as well as provide evidence of the other person's wrong. The goal is that we may communicate and reason together, to establish resolution and reconciliation. It also provides the opportunity for repentance and forgiveness, wherever it may be applicable to those involved.

Bitterness rejects help and is unrepentant

Some people still do not respond despite all efforts to help them repent and be reconciled. If the person in my illustration refuses to repent, we must acknowledge his decision. We understand that someone who does not desire to be reconciled to the person who has been offended has his own personal issues which have caused bitterness to take root in his life. In all likelihood, that bitterness has started to pollute others. We do not hate him, but we must put him outside the church for the safety of others in the body, otherwise his attitude will affect them.

We now gently exclude him from fellowship until he is ready to repent, to make right and be reconciled. If he is willing to repent, then we can deal with it. Until then he is outside the church's fellowship, behind a wall of separation which he has built for himself through his own bitterness.

Whatever the other person does, I must apply God's Word on forgiveness to the situation. He may not repent, but I still must forgive him. While he remains unrepentant, I must not hold him in unforgiveness until he does repent. That would be quite wrong. We still put him outside the church, and wait for him. If later he says that he is really sorry and he wants to be restored, I am able to embrace and accept him back because I have already forgiven him.

If I have not forgiven him, my attitude will cause me to think, 'Good riddance! We don't ever want to see you again, so stay away!' Because I have not dealt with unforgiveness in my heart, the bruise I took now becomes bitterness. I don't want reconciliation, but at the same time I resent the fact that the person concerned will not be reconciled to me, and will not repent, so I reject him. The biblical principle is that we must forgive everyone unconditionally, even when people are not willing to repent. This is because whenever we forgive anyone, we release them to God and to His better judgment.

This does not only apply to one another within the body of Christ. God's principles are equally relevant and applicable to all, friends, neighbours and those in our workplace. Whatever the relationship, God's desire is for us to walk in righteousness and truth, being witnesses to His compassion and forgiving heart.

Use the examples provided in this chapter to help you identify any bitterness in your heart. Your speech, actions, behaviour and attitudes will provide indicators if there is. The consequences of bitterness are serious. Do all you can to be at peace with everyone.

PART TWO
DEALING WITH THE DESTRUCTIVE NATURE OF UNFORGIVENESS

CHAPTER FOUR

HOW UNFORGIVENESS DESTROYS LIVES

Have you ever wondered exactly why unforgiveness is such a destructive force? Many of its characteristics are not widely recognised or understood. Once identified, they help explain its power and significance in your life and your need to become and remain free from it.

Unforgiveness binds us to the past

When we make an accusation against someone and do not forgive them, we, in effect, imprison them in our unforgiveness. As a result we become bound to the past where the issue occurred. It is not the situation itself that binds us to the past, but how we have dealt with that situation and person spiritually and emotionally.

For example, when you were a child, your father may never have acknowledged you or told you that he loved you. Although that may be the truth of the situation, you are not bound to the past by what actually happened. You are not imprisoned by the **fact** that your father never showed you his approval. But you are bound to it because of the impact it had on you as a result of how you dealt with it.

Trauma does not have to traumatise. This becomes evident when you recognise that two people can experience the same trauma, with the same potential to hurt and bruise, but not become affected in the same way. If one forgives and the other does not, their lives will take totally different directions. The one who forgives is able to walk away from the past hurt and pain, to live in the freedom of forgiveness and live a productive life. In contrast, the one who does not forgive is bound to the past, trapped in the hurt and pain of unforgiveness, which limits his ability to function productively in most areas of his life.

We can also be bound to the past by our perception or belief concerning what happened. I have known people stay hurt for years because they believed they were being rejected, unloved, ignored and ridiculed, etc. when there was absolutely no evidence in reality. Their belief was based solely on their perception, whether through misunderstanding, insecurity or deception. Although the event was seen through the filter of their imagination as hurtful, and wasn't in fact that way, it still caused as much hurt and pain as if it had really happened. By contrast, some people may actually be rejected, unloved, ignored, ridiculed or mistreated in some other way, yet refuse to allow that reality to affect them negatively. As a result, they are not bruised and they avoid the hurt and pain that would otherwise have bound them to their past.

Whether the cause of hurt is through a belief about something that actually happened, or a belief about something that never took place, it is unforgiveness that binds people to the past and affects their present and future lives. That is how powerful unforgiveness is.

Unforgiveness binds us to people

The problem with hurt that binds us to the past is that we are unable to live fully in the present. Many of our present situations have become contaminated by the past, even though we may not recognise it, or if we do, we do not know why.

Where there's unforgiveness, our hurts bind us to the person whose words or actions hurt us. So, while we are carrying a hurt, every time a situation arises that reminds us of it, it also reminds us of that person. This indicates that we have become emotionally bound to them and they have become part of our lives.

To illustrate this, suppose you are getting married. If unforgiveness is in you, it will not just be you and your spouse in your marriage. There are others entering the wedding ceremony with you. These are all the people you have not forgiven from your past. They are all present with you at the altar, because you are still holding on to them in unforgiveness. However, both you and the person you are marrying are totally unaware of their presence. They may not be physically there, but they are present in you, imprisoned in your unforgiveness. They go on honeymoon with you; in effect, they live with you as long as you hold them in unforgiveness. This also means that the marriage may suffer many unnecessary and unhelpful challenges because of your invisible residents, not to mention Satan who's become a squatter through the opportunity you have given him.

Unforgiveness prevents us receiving and giving love

Many people who struggle with giving and receiving love are in that position because they are still carrying hurts from the past. When we have been hurt or rejected and have not dealt with it, we employ many different mechanisms to protect ourselves from further hurt and bruising. As I mentioned earlier, some people withdraw, whereas others may become unpleasant or even aggressive. Not only that; the mere fact of not forgiving seriously disables us in regard to loving and being loved.

Love, by its nature, requires an open heart unsullied by the grime of hurt, rejection, resentment, anger and unforgiveness. Love is pure because it is of God. *No one has seen God at any time. If we love one another, God abides in us, and His love has been perfected in us. 1 John 4:12.* It should be abundantly clear by now from what I have already said, that God's love and forgiveness will not be expressed in and through our lives while we hold someone in unforgiveness. For a Christian, that is a serious handicap.

Unforgiveness binds us to a life of torment

I explained earlier that if you choose not to forgive someone, you imprison them in your unforgiveness. It's actually worse than that. Because you refused to forgive them you made it known that you were not willing to let God deal with their lives as the righteous Judge of all men. You set up your own judicial system in which you charged them, found them guilty, sentenced them and put them in your jail of unforgiveness. You became prosecutor, judge and jailer.

Then, because you imprisoned them, as jailer you have the responsibility of keeping them there. You continue to feed them on your failure to forgive because of your hurt and pain. Bound to them in this way, you are no longer free to do as you please. You are on permanent prison duty; you cannot take time out to do as you please or to go on holiday, because wherever you go, they go.

Prison is a very unpleasant place. There is shouting and wailing because it is a place of torment. It is impossible to have a peaceful night's sleep, because prisoners wake you up in the middle of the night banging their cage begging you to let them out. In a similar way, unforgiveness can lead to a troubled mind, disturbed sleep and an unsettled heart. Unforgiveness binds you to your own inner disturbance, as though in prison yourself. Just as the prisoner is bound, so unforgiveness imprisons you and binds you to a life of torment. The memory of the hurt and the retaining of the bruise and bitterness continually hold you in the pain of the past and you are unable to live free from it in the present.

My wife and I have two little dogs, which provide me with an illustration. I am not saying that they are a torment, but we are now responsible for them. This means that when we want to go away even for a few days, we have to stop and consider who is going to take care of them. Previously we would just take our suitcases, lock the front door and go, but now we have to think of the dogs. We have to find somebody to feed them and look after them; otherwise they must go with us on holiday.

That is exactly what happens with unforgiveness. You are no longer free to go and do as you please because you cannot leave your unforgiveness behind while you take a break. No one can or will volunteer for the job of taking care of those you have imprisoned. This is how unforgiveness holds you captive.

Unforgiveness retains the other person's sin in our lives

The destructive power of unforgiveness does not stop at binding you to the past and to the people of the past. It's not just a matter of torment. As long as you do not forgive the person you consider hurt you, they are still in their sin as far as your justice system is concerned. They are guilty of sinning against you and as far as you are concerned they can stay in the prison of your unforgiveness. You will not forgive their sin!

Here I need to make something quite clear. It is God and God alone who can forgive sins. He did not transfer that authority to anyone. All men must repent of their own sin towards God in order to be saved and continue to be saved through life and into eternity. The forgiveness we are talking about here is what is necessary for you to release that person from your prison and into the hands of God. This is for the sake of your freedom from bondage to the person you have held in unforgiveness.

This principle is seen in this passage of scripture when the resurrected Jesus met with His disciples: *He breathed on them, and said to them, "Receive the Holy Spirit. If you forgive the sins of any, they are forgiven them; if you retain the sins of any, they are retained." John 20:22-23.* These were some of the earliest recorded words that Jesus spoke to His disciples after His resurrection, which is an indication of how important He considered them.

Until we are born again and have the nature of God in us, we do not have the capacity to forgive. Our sin nature does not have that capacity. Forgiveness is an expression of the love of God. It is when God abides in us and can express Himself through us that true forgiveness becomes possible. Having been born of the Spirit we have the capacity to forgive. But it also follows, if we then choose not to forgive, we retain that sin and continue to imprison that person in our unforgiveness as well as imprison ourselves. We are no longer free to live the life which God planned, purposed and purchased for us through the blood of Christ Jesus.

Don't let the destructiveness of unforgiveness reside in your life. Recognise how important it is to forgive others. Remain free from chaining yourself to situations and people of the past. Take responsibility for your own sin. Do not retain others in their sin. As a born again believer let the nature of God be revealed in you through a life of love and forgiveness.

CHAPTER FIVE

REVERSING THE DESTRUCTION CAUSED BY UNFORGIVENESS

Now that you are able to identify unforgiveness in your life, let us examine some key principles which will help you in the process of reversing its devastating effects.

Expose the situation where hurt became embedded in your life

When deep hurt has occurred, patterns of behaviour associated with unforgiveness will be evident, unless we choose to ignore them and pretend they are not there. Then we have to go on living with them. However, in order to reverse the destruction caused by unforgiveness and walk free from the hurt and pain, it is necessary to remind ourselves of what happened to bring that hurt into our lives.

Thinking about situations or people that caused feelings of hurt is not something we naturally want to do. It is quite understandable that we may want to avoid them altogether. However, it is important for us to bring each situation to our remembrance in order to find where we allowed bruising and unforgiveness to come in. We must expose the situation and understand it so that we can deal with it properly.

Don't be tempted to accuse others and blame them for your response to what happened. This is something the devil would love you to do.

Blaming others means you're not willing to take responsibility for your part, the situation cannot be resolved and the devil can still have access to your life. What you need to face up to is that when you chose not to forgive the person who caused you your hurt, you stood as judge over them, and in so doing, you acted as though you were God. You then succumbed to the most fundamental temptation the devil puts before anyone, that is, to be 'like' God. "For God knows that in the day you eat of it your eyes will be opened, and you will be like God, knowing good and evil." (Genesis 3:5.)

You have no right to negative feelings about others

When we experience painful situations, we are easily persuaded that we have a right to our negative feelings and the bitterness that arises in unforgiveness. But the truth we all must face up to is that we do not have that right.

You may find this very hard to accept. You might have experienced pain and hurt for many years. When such suffering was in response to what someone else did or said, what I am saying may not seem fair, or not even seem to make sense to you just yet. But please recognise that I am saying this to help you break free from all that suffering and help you do it God's way.

You must reckon with the fact that you only have a right to deal with your own life. Forgiveness requires you to forfeit the right you thought you had to hold on to negative feelings about others. While you hold on to that right as you see it, you are neither in a position to release the person to God, nor be released from the prison you have made for yourself through unforgiveness.

Judging brings God's judgment on you

I have already spoken to you in chapter four about how you become prosecutor, judge and jailer in your own judicial system through unforgiveness. I have told you that in doing this you did something which you had no right to do. God alone is the righteous Judge.

What you must now reckon with is that because you judged others, you are judged by God.

Let us revise something we have already spoken about. Jesus, when instructing His disciples, revealed something important concerning what our attitude should be towards other people: *"Love your enemies, do good, and lend, hoping for nothing in return...." Luke 6:35.* Here we see that Jesus tells us not to expect a return for doing what is right. As we mentioned before, if our expectations are for a return and if that is unfulfilled, it can lead to hurt and bitterness. So, Jesus instructs His disciples not to hope for anything in return. Even so, there is a reward, but we still have to live as those who are merciful and forgive.

Jesus continued: *"And your reward will be great, and you will be sons of the Most High. For He is kind to the unthankful and evil."* If God is kind to the unthankful and evil, how dare we judge them? We should follow the advice Jesus gives: *"Therefore be merciful, just as your Father also is merciful. Judge not, and you shall not be judged. Condemn not, and you shall not be condemned. Forgive, and you will be forgiven." Luke 6:36-37.*

You may have set up your justice system for others, but the truth is that in God's justice system, you stand in the dock in His courtroom. According to scripture, you are the guilty one against whom the charge is brought and being found guilty, you are the prisoner.

Therefore the first move you must take towards your freedom is to repent to God and seek His forgiveness for setting yourself up to be like God. You did what you had no right to do. Until you deal with what you have done, you will not be able to forgive the other person as God requires because your relationship with Him is out of order and must first be restored. It is out of that relationship that you have the capacity to forgive; otherwise you are locked into that unforgiveness and the consequences of unforgiveness won't go away.

Repent and ask God to forgive you. You must align yourself with God's order in which He and He alone is the righteous Judge. He alone knows the true condition of a person's heart. You don't. To repent is your choice. It requires an act of your will to do what is right before God. Then it follows that you must deal with the unforgiveness itself and release the person you hold in unforgiveness to God's better judgment.

In getting things right, let us not fall into temptation

Having humbled ourselves before God and received His forgiveness, we must continue in the same spirit. We must deal with the unforgiveness itself and release the person we have imprisoned to God's better judgment. We must also, as far as we can, help the other person get things right with God.

Galatians 6:1 teaches us how to do this and what our attitude and response should be towards someone whose sin affects us: *Brethren, if a man is overtaken in any trespass, you who are spiritual restore such a one in a spirit of gentleness, considering yourself lest you also be tempted.*

The principle of restoration is clearly explained here by Paul for our own benefit as well as that of others. His instruction includes a warning to us: when we restore others, we need to do it in such a way that we do not become tempted. Tempted to do what? To hurt them as they hurt us because our approach was not in the spirit of gentleness. There is no room for pride, superiority or self-righteousness.

If believers would only heed Paul's instruction, it would avoid untold pain and suffering. Sadly, all too often, we observe the behaviour of others and think that we would never do what they have done. What we do not consider is that through this attitude, we continue as prosecutor, judge and jailor. Then, maybe even years later, we suddenly realise to our dismay that we are doing the very same thing we judged to be so wrong and vowed we would never do.

Words which reveal keys to our freedom

When it comes to the matter of actually forgiving someone, we need a biblical understanding of what forgiveness means. We must forgive God's way. If we don't, forgiving and being forgiven will be ineffective and will not produce biblical results. We therefore need to examine our own perceptions and recognise how they have been formed.

English dictionaries define forgiveness as meaning: 'cease to feel angry or bitter towards someone or about an offence'. This is the essence of what is widely taught and accepted as the correct definition. If you have tried to implement forgiveness on this basis and not succeeded, you are not alone. Your understanding and lack of success have been subject to the limitations of the definitions we have accepted. This does not portray the whole truth of God's Word. Our own efforts, without applying God's Word, will never achieve God's righteous purposes.

When we study the word 'forgiveness' in its biblical context, we discover that the roots of the word in the Greek reveal many facets and meanings. These provide us with a wider and deeper perception. There are two Greek words which help our understanding of the biblical concept of forgiveness and bring us to the point where we can truly forgive. These words are:

> 'Apoluo', which means: 'to forgive, to set free, to liberate one from a thing' or 'to let go, to release.'
>
> 'Aphiami', which means: 'to forgive, let go or to send away' and, even more importantly, 'to cancel, to remit, to pardon.'

The following example shows the use of apoluo as 'forgive'. It's found in Luke's parallel passage to Matthew's Sermon on the Mount: "*Judge not [neither pronouncing judgment nor subjecting to censure], and you will not be judged; do not condemn and pronounce guilty, and you will not be condemned and pronounced guilty; acquit and forgive and release (give up resentment, let it drop), and you will be acquitted and forgiven and released." Luke 6:37 Amplified Bible.*

In this amplified scripture, three words become particularly significant for us: acquit, forgive and release. These words help us greatly to understand the process of forgiveness. 'Acquit' means to drop the charge; 'forgive' means to wipe out the offence, and 'release' means to set free. When a charge is dropped against someone, the offence is wiped out and they are released and set free.

What I am about to explain may at first seem a strange concept. However, it is vitally important in helping you break free from the influences that have held you captive.

Remember, you have been your own prosecutor, judge and jailer in regard to the life of another. Having recognised this and repented towards God to receive His forgiveness, you are then in a position to forgive and release the person you have imprisoned in your unforgiveness.

To do this you must first cancel the charge you raised against them as prosecutor. In effect you must become the other person's defence lawyer in order to appeal to the righteous Judge to have the charge you brought cancelled. You must plead a case on their behalf to cancel what you have done.

Let's suppose it was your parents who you held in unforgiveness. You come before God and say something like this: "Lord God, I confess that I wrongly charged Mum and Dad with what I considered a sin against me. In truth, I didn't and still don't really know why what happened occurred in the first place. I did not know what was in their hearts. Forgive me, Lord God, for holding them in unforgiveness and having a bad attitude towards them. Whatever happened, I had no right to judge them, for you are the only true Judge. My Mum and Dad are your responsibility to deal with, not mine. I forgive them in Jesus' name and I release them to you and no longer hold anything against them."

You have asked God to cancel the charge you wrongly brought against them. You confessed that you had no right to do that, that you're not God and never knew the whole truth behind the situation. You asked for His forgiveness for having held them in unforgiveness. You then forgave them, let them go, and released them to God as the only one who can legitimately address the situation with regard to your parents. It is, and always was, up to your parents to deal with the situation by going to God on their own behalf. You just leave them with God.

This may seem particularly difficult while you are still hurting. It may seem very unfair. But it is God's righteous way and in responding accordingly, He will bring healing to your heart and life. You will be released from the prison where you put yourself through unforgiveness.

Remember, the charges brought against Jesus were wholly unjust and no-one had the right to bring them against Him. Yet He did not judge His accusers, but appealed to the Father on their behalf. *"Father, forgive them, for they do not know what they do." Luke 23:34.* This is worth remembering always, especially when we think that to forgive is unfair and seemingly unjust because of what others have done. If Jesus had not been prepared to forgive others, despite Himself being without sin, His death would not have been an acceptable sacrifice for sin before God, and we would be without hope.

What we do by dealing with our hurt and unforgiveness is to put things back into order in our lives. Then we can again know the peace of God which passes all understanding. *Be anxious for nothing, but in everything by prayer and supplication, with thanksgiving, let your requests be made known to God; and the peace of God, which surpasses all understanding, will guard your hearts and minds through Christ Jesus. (Philippians 4:6-7.)*

When we forgive, the Holy Spirit washes and cleanses us and heals the hurt, frees us from the torment and restores our relationship with the Father. We are then in a position to function in the fullness of God's purpose for our lives, growing and maturing as children of God.

Church must be a place where forgiveness prevails

As members of the body of Christ, the church, the need to walk in forgiveness must permeate every aspect of our lives for the sake of the church of which we are members. For example, a church leader may have well-defined views on what he expects from his worship leader. What happens if one day the worship leader doesn't turn up for the service?

In all probability, after the initial shock, he is tempted to get upset, annoyed, angry and confrontational. Then accusing words and unfounded judgments may roll off his lips. It's likely that others will get caught in the crossfire. He's hurt and is reluctant to forgive because he's been so messed about by what he sees as the worship leader's irresponsible behaviour.

Then he may try and take over the worship leader's role. The team becomes unsettled. Church members find his inconsistencies and efforts affect the spiritual and administrative dynamics of church, and so it goes on. Yes, this sort of thing has happened in churches, and similar things do happen across the church. The detail may be different, but the faltering dynamic and unsettling of the body is much the same.

The whole situation could have been approached differently, with mercy, care, concern and a heart to help the worship leader that would make it possible for him to fulfil his role and calling. And this would have been for everyone's benefit.

This sort of situation can be translated into so many areas where relationships are challenged and tested. A heart of mercy that is ready to forgive and release is a fundamental requirement of any Christian. But when our flesh nature creeps in and reacts with hurt instead of responding with mercy, all manner of consequences flow out to other people and the devil rides upon it to create chaos, division and destroy the work of God. This is the complete opposite of what Jesus came to do. *For this purpose the Son of God was manifested, that He might destroy the works of the devil. 1 John 3:8.*

Violence, abuse, crime, anger or any offensiveness against you is not God's will and we can say quite rightly that it should not happen. However, regardless of whatever incidents brought you to the place of making that accusation which led to unforgiveness, God in His love and mercy for you wants to release you from all the pain, hurt, suffering and disappointment. In order to achieve that, you need to understand and be prepared to continue in the process of restoration that He has begun in you.

A word for children and young people

Sometimes young people are hurt and offended by what they perceive their parents have said or done or not done. Some grow up still carrying the hurt and unforgiveness. Some take issue and the parent and child relationship breaks down with all sorts of unhappy results. Then the child or young person has a moment in which they think they will be magnanimous and go to their parents and say, "I forgive you," and walk away feeling good about it. But they haven't understood the uniqueness of the parent and child relationship and in so doing have contradicted the Word of God.

What they did in being magnanimous was in fact arrogance because it was an open admission that they have judged their father or mother. Their response was more like a conqueror coming to a defeated foe than coming in the spirit of Christ. Not only through unforgiveness have they imprisoned their parents in the first place, but their 'I forgive you' response is out of order. The Bible says that children are to honour and respect their parents *(Ephesians 6:2)*, not honour and correct. The right attitude would be to humble themselves before God and say, "God forgive me for judging my father and mother. I'm supposed to honour them, so Lord I'm going to honour them, and I release them to You."

No matter what the circumstances may have been, no-one should ever criticise their parents. No-one should tell their mother or father that they had a terrible childhood or that their parents disciplined them too hard. No parents should ever be confronted or accused by their own children with all the wrong things they were judged to have done. If you identify with this situation, go to your parents and thank them for giving you life. Thank them for every positive thing you can. Remember the good things they did and said. If all you can do is thank them for giving you life, then do that.

Don't hesitate to deal with unforgiveness; it is such a destructive thing. God has provided a way for you to be released from its bondage and into the freedom He has provided. Get right with God and live again. You are a member of the body of Christ, the church. Sanctify yourself and let God build His church through you and the rest of the saints.

CHAPTER SIX

MOVING ON INTO GOD'S ORDER

Once the issues of unforgiveness have been dealt with and your relationship with God restored so that His nature in you can direct your life to fulfil His purposes for you, life must continue that way. We need to constantly check that our heart is free from unforgiveness and that sin has not crept in again.

Be reassured that in order to forgive, you are not required to deny the facts that caused the hurt and pain. Unless you were mistaken or deceived, the facts were what they were. Any sinful behaviour was sinful. But whatever the facts, we must forgive and let God deal with the situation as only He can. He is righteous altogether. *(Psalm 19:9.)* He knows what's in a man's heart, and He knows what's in your heart, whether there's bitterness and unforgiveness. What we must concern ourselves with is that we live before God in His love and with a merciful and forgiving heart. Let us live as Jesus exhorted us: *"But I say to you, love your enemies, bless those who curse you, do good to those who hate you, and pray for those who spitefully use you and persecute you, that you may be sons of your Father in heaven; for He makes His sun rise on the evil and on the good, and sends rain on the just and on the unjust." Matthew 5:44-45.*

Move on in the freedom of forgiveness

When you asked God to forgive you, when you chose to forgive others no matter what had happened, God reversed the destruction that unforgiveness had brought into your life. He restored you spiritually and emotionally and you were able to shut the door on the devil and all his works. Now it's a matter of choice that you continue to live in the freedom of forgiveness and fulfil the life that God has given you. Continue to allow God to deal with the sin in your life. Don't give it time to settle.

Then treat both yourself and others as forgiven. Forgiveness is love in action. See your life through God's eyes and thank Him for it. Realise that God cared about you all the time, whatever may have happened. Remind yourself that your heavenly Father loves you and always keeps watch over you, taking care of you and leading you in the paths of righteousness. *(Psalm 23:3.)*

Make a point of reading *1 Corinthians 13:1-8* and see how love behaves. When we apply this wisdom to our lives, we will not judge the person for what they do, but we can confront the fruit of that person's behaviour, which in fact may have been quite wrong. We do not pretend their sin is not sin. We do not call that which is evil as though it is good, no more than we call that which is good as though it is evil. We may have to deal with the consequences of their behaviour and may even have to help the person correct it. But as believers in whom Christ dwells, we will receive that person with an open heart that is merciful and forgives.

The purpose of forgiveness is for the restoration of the bride

The work of the Holy Spirit is in order to purify and sanctify your heart, so that you can fulfil your potential as one called out by God. Only the Holy Spirit can do this, and it is a crucial part of God's plan and purpose for mankind. But there is a bigger picture. You are part of the church, the body of Christ, and it is fundamental and vital that you are able to function effectively as part of that body.

God's ultimate purpose of forgiveness is for the restoration and purification of His bride, the church. We read that Christ *loved the church and gave Himself for her, that He might sanctify and cleanse her with the washing of water by the word, that He might present her to Himself a glorious church, not having spot or wrinkle or any such thing, but that she should be holy and without blemish. Ephesians 5:25-27.*

The church is not a building where believers go every Sunday. The church is God's people, born-again believers who have Jesus Christ living in them. The building is just a facility in which to meet. That is why we must allow Him to purify us and sanctify us, and why we must be quick to forgive others as He has forgiven us; because we are the church.

Why did it happen to me?

When referring back to the situation which caused them so much hurt and pain, people often ask me this question in one form or another: if God was watching over me, why did that awful situation happen to me? Why did He allow it to happen? A good question and one which is not difficult for me to answer and explain and for people to understand.

When God made man in His own image, He gave him the freedom to act independently. We call this free moral choice. But with this freedom came responsibility, the responsibility to do what is right towards God and others. When man embraced the devil's temptation to reach out and be like God, he grasped the opportunity to have both the knowledge of good and evil. In this way sin entered into man and he was separated from the presence of God. As a result, he readily made choices for selfish gain. This meant that he would go on rebelling against God. One of the results of this was that he could cause other people pain in their lives spiritually, emotionally and physically.

It is because of this we need to be born again. Through sin, man is in no position to do what is right before God. However, as born again believers our way of life is clear. This is what Jesus said: *You shall love the Lord your God with all your heart, with all your soul, and with all your mind* and *You shall love your neighbour as yourself. Matthew 22:37, 39.* Luke also quotes Jesus as saying: *Just as you want men to do to you, you also do to them likewise. Luke 6:31.* That is the way of life in the kingdom of God which we have entered as believers; and by the grace of God through faith we have the ability to live that way.

Consider your relationship with God

In order for you to move on in your life, there is a vital consideration concerning your relationship with God.

If you were once close to God, but you have let that relationship grow cold, perhaps because of hurt, disappointment or a broken relationship, you need to repent and return to Him right now. While you stay away from your heavenly Father, you are rejecting Him and His forgiveness. Until you return to Him and receive His forgiveness, you will not have His power and ability within you to make it possible for you to forgive and release others.

If you don't draw near to Him, not only are you risking God's most precious gift of your salvation, you also are missing out on all the blessings of the freedom He has for you; you are missing out on your earthly destiny in your life now.

Your heavenly Father is waiting for you to return to Him. He wants you to have your full inheritance as His beloved child and heir. But first you need to repent and ask God to forgive you for walking away from Him. If you know you don't have a close relationship with Him and you want to return to Him, then pray this prayer with all sincerity in your heart:

Prayer of recommitment

"Heavenly Father, I recognise that I have become distracted and drawn away from my relationship with you. I have sinned. I have rejected your love for me. I repent and turn back from my self-centred living and ask you to forgive me. I recommit my life to you now and ask you to help me live close to you and in the way you desire for me. Enable me by your Holy Spirit to be empowered to live in the blessings and the destiny that you have already prepared for me. I thank you Father God that you forgive me and I can now live in the liberty by which Christ has made me free, and I will not be entangled again with a yoke of bondage. *(Galatians 5:1.)* Amen."

You must be born again

You may have been going to church for a long time, you may consider yourself to be a 'good' person, or that you are doing great things for God. None of these things in themselves make you a Christian. The only thing that makes you a Christian is having an intimate relationship with God through Jesus, His Son.

If you do not know Jesus as your Lord and Saviour, if you do not know God as your heavenly Father, God wants you to put that right so that you can be reconciled to Him and enjoy the blessings of being a child of God. Becoming a Christian is not about joining a church or a denomination, but about an eternal family relationship with the Creator and of all mankind. It is a love relationship: *"God so loved the world that He gave His only begotten Son, that whoever believes in Him should not perish but have everlasting life." John 3:16.*

Jesus is the doorway to that everlasting life. God wants to place His Spirit in you so that you can receive everything He longs to give you. The first step to this glorious life is that you must be born again by His Spirit and allow Jesus to come and live in you. How do you do that? You need to pray a simple prayer, trusting that God's grace will save you from your sin and establish you as His child. I invite you now to say this out loud, with sincerity:

Prayer of salvation

"Heavenly Father, I recognise that I have not had a relationship with you and that I've thought I could do things in my own strength and in my own way. I repent of living my life without you and I ask you to forgive me.

"I believe that Jesus Christ is the Son of God and that He died in my place for my sin, that I might be forgiven. I thank you that He rose again from the dead to prove that He is God and to enable me to live as a child of God. I believe that He is able to give me a new life and whatever I need to live as you have planned and purposed for me.

"I receive Jesus now into my life as Lord and Saviour. I thank you that you have heard my prayer and that you have come into my life as you said you would. I receive your forgiveness and count myself as set free from my sin. I thank you that you will lead me and help me in my relationship with you and that with your help I will be able to live in a right relationship towards all other people, with your love in me. I pray this in the name of Jesus. Amen."

Being reconciled to God is the most important thing in life. Jesus died for us so that we could be reconciled to Him. Now you must set your focus on God your heavenly Father and His purpose for your life, living in the freedom of His forgiveness and forgiving others as He has forgiven you.

PART THREE
FORGIVING YOURSELF

CHAPTER SEVEN

THE MOST SIGNIFICANT PERSON IN YOUR LIFE

Who is the most significant person in your life? Who do you think has had the greatest impact and made the biggest difference to you? Everyone can think of someone who has played an important role in their life. The majority of believers would probably say that it was Jesus. What would you say?

I am about to describe someone you need to know, understand, respect and love. If you fail to see this person like that, you will not relate very well to anybody, because this particular individual holds the key to all your relationships. What you think about this person is therefore vitally important and has particular relevance to the whole area of forgiving.

The most significant person in your life is **you**. Like many people who have been hurt, you may not know or accept that, but until you do, you will not fully understand and experience the freedom of forgiveness.

Do not be your own worst enemy

J. Martin Cohen wrote about an explorer who went into the wilds of Africa, taking trinkets and two full length mirrors with him for the natives of the land. He placed the mirrors against two trees and sat down to talk to some of the men about the exploration. At the same time, the explorer watched as a warrior with a spear in his hand approached a mirror. The warrior looked into the mirror and immediately smashed it to pieces with his spear.

The explorer was very surprised at this violent reaction towards his gift to the natives. He walked over to the warrior and asked him why he had smashed the mirror. The man replied, "He go kill me; I kill him first."

From the explorer's view point, the scene he had witnessed was one of inexplicable destruction. The warrior's point of view, however, was that his act was necessary self-defence. When the warrior looked into the mirror, with a spear in his hand, he saw a man he did not know or recognise, also with a spear in his hand. In the warrior's mind, he was attacking an armed opponent in order to save his own life. He was unaware that he was attacking his own reflection.

This illustrates what we may do to ourselves if we don't see ourselves as God sees us. We attack the reflection of who we think we are. Often the view we have of ourselves is erroneous and we bring destruction by our faulty thinking. This is why, when it comes to relationships, many of our problems are caused from being our own worst enemy. We also blame the devil for so much that he is not even involved in, and we do not realise that we ourselves are responsible for our distress.

Be who God created you to be

When we spend time focused on our problems, they begin to form our identity. This then prevents us from being delivered from those problems. We even go so far as wanting to hold on to them because they give us a sense of value and a sense of who we are.

It is not God's will that our problems define who we are. When we know and accept what God created us to be, our problems will never define us again. He wants us to rise above our burdens and problems, to live in the freedom He has purchased for us. But through our wrong thinking we can keep ourselves out of the kingdom of God and the joy of God's blessings.

Repent from dead works

One of the results of living with a wrong view of yourself is that you live life based on your own wisdom and do things in your own strength instead of trusting God. When you fail to recognise the importance of trusting God in everything, you invite more trouble into your life than you can imagine. The effect of this is that your works are dead, your efforts at doing what's right have no life in them, they are of no effect and do not produce what God wants for your life.

This means that you must repent from your dead works *(Hebrews 6:1)*. Turn away from trying to solve your own problems, inadequacies and lack of goodness. Turn to God in everything, tell Him that you need Him, that you want His help to sort out every aspect of your life. Let Him lead you so you can live life to the full as He intended and embrace everything that God has made you to be.

Know your value

If we are to become who God wants us to be, we must know how to feel good about ourselves. Many Christians talk about their problems endlessly - and everything else that has captivated them - whenever they open their mouths. Most believers know how to bring themselves down and how to beat themselves up. Some even think it is sin to feel good about themselves. They do not realise who they really are, or recognise their true value.

Everything God creates is good. He created you with the uttermost thought and attention to detail. He put the package together and you were born, a unique person, precious to God. David recognised this is what God did for him and voiced his thanks and praise: *You formed my inward parts; You covered me in my mother's womb. I will praise You, for I am fearfully and wonderfully made.... Psalm 139:13-14.* If you find fault with yourself, you find fault with the one who created you.

Years ago I stopped criticising myself and started to embrace who God created me to be. I have never been more fulfilled, more complete or more blessed. I say 'blessed' rather than 'happy' because blessed means to be favoured by God, but the root word of 'happy' is based on chance. When you are blessed by God, 'chance' is not involved. God deals in certainties. You are in a God-ordained position and condition.

You may find this hard to accept. You may not like certain aspects about yourself. Perhaps you think that you're too tall, too short, too fat, too thin, and so on. While you are finding fault with yourself, you will never take pleasure in being you and you will never enjoy your differences. By the way, the things you feel critical about could be the very things that someone else appreciates. What you think is 'abnormal' is probably quite normal. But the way you choose to look at things will govern you.

Glorify God and feel good about yourself

God expects you to feel good about yourself. This is not only because He made you, but also because it glorifies Him and His creation. I am not talking about a narcissistic kind of self-love, but about feeling pleased with who God created you to be.

I have so many reasons every day to thank God for making me who I am. One very simple reason is this, which I am sure many men will identify with: every morning it takes more than an hour for my wife Michelle to prepare for the day, but I only need fifteen minutes. There is no way I would want to subject myself to all the things she puts herself through; the cleansing, tweaking, tweezing, doing all those things that ladies do. All this is part of who Michelle is, and we each rejoice in who God made us to be.

God wants you to have a healthy respect for yourself. The word 'respect' means: to show consideration for, to admire, to value, to have high regard for, appreciate and esteem. Tragically, when most of us look in the mirror we want to change the reflection we see there because we do not have respect for who God created us to be.

Understand the command to love

Someone once said that if you do not have respect for yourself, your neighbour is in serious trouble. Paul talked about this and showed how true that statement is: *You, brethren, have been called to liberty; only do not use liberty as an opportunity for the flesh, but through love serve one another. For all the law is fulfilled in one word, even in this: "You shall love your neighbour as yourself." But if you bite and devour one another, beware lest you be consumed by one another! Galatians 5:13-15.* If I do not love myself as God has made me, then any attempt to love others is undermined by my self-criticism. It is hypocrisy to tell someone I love them when I do not love myself as God intended. If I 'bite and devour' others, it's a sure sign that my self-criticism is spilling over to them.

The command to love is vitally important because it is through love for God and others that we can fulfil the commands of God. This is exactly what Jesus explained to the Pharisees and Sadducees when one of them asked Him which the great commandment was in the Law: *"'You shall love the Lord your God with all your heart, with all your soul, and with all your mind.' This is the first and great commandment. And the second is like it: 'You shall love your neighbour as yourself.' On these two commandments hang all the Law and the Prophets." Matthew 22:37-40.*

It is not difficult to see that the second commandment is a natural consequence of the first. This means, if we are having difficulty with the second, it's quite likely we're not doing too well as far as the first command is concerned. And if we do not see ourselves as God does, we are certainly having difficulty with the first.

The first commandment, loving God, is a challenge. It requires a decision to obey God by loving Him that way; it doesn't depend on our feelings. Often our greatest challenge is exposed through the second commandment, especially when it comes to loving ourselves. We cannot reverse the order of this principle. We cannot love our neighbour first and hope to love ourselves as a result. It begins first from within, from loving God and who you are, loving who God created **you** to be. It begins with becoming content and fulfilled in that. Only then can you truly love others.

It is absolutely impossible to love anyone else if you do not love who God created you to be. You will begin to break down, devour, hurt and offend others, because hurt and offended people hurt people. When this happens, we justify our behaviour, believing it is because of what other people have done to us. The real reason we hurt others is because of what is lacking within us. We lack the respect that we should have for ourselves, for who God created us to be, for the gifts, abilities and talents that God put in us.

Change is made possible when we understand and apply the command to love in the correct order: love God, then ourselves, then others. Until that order is established, we remain inadequate within ourselves, biting and devouring others.

Stop being your own worst enemy and start being who God created you to be. Know your value, respect yourself and glorify God by feeling good about yourself. Finally, and of most importance, understand and obey the command to love, so that God's love flows to you and through you to others.

CHAPTER EIGHT

FORGIVE YOURSELF AND TAKE HOLD OF YOUR FREEDOM

Sometimes it seems hard to break from the destructive influences of the past. Some believers find they are still caught in the cycle of being hurt and hurting others. This stumbling block must be overcome if you want to move on and experience the freedom God has prepared for you.

Understand why you find it hard to forgive yourself

Before you can reach the point of forgiving yourself, you need to recognise what holds you back. You can be the hardest person to forgive. Most people find it far easier to forgive someone else than they do to forgive themselves. This is because they become their own prosecutor, judge, and jailor as they continue to inflict blow after blow upon themselves.

Often we have a tendency to re-visit our past failures in our minds and emotions. Whenever a situation arises that remotely reminds us of something that previously hurt us, the memories cause us to experience the same pain and suffering. We go over and over in our minds what we said or what we should have said, what we did or what we should have done, what the other person said or did, and so on. This cycle replays continually and we cannot forgive ourselves.

Can you identify with this? Are there things you blame yourself for and have never forgiven yourself for? When you are not willing to forgive yourself, you make yourself greater than God and then there is nobody who can help you. I say this because until you receive forgiveness from God and apply that forgiveness to your life and forgive yourself, you cannot forgive others and release them so you can enjoy your freedom.

You keep setting yourself up as prosecutor; you repeatedly bring the accusation, the charge, against yourself. Then you act as the judge and find yourself guilty. As a result, you become your jailer, placing yourself in the prison of your unforgiveness. And there you will stay until you get this right with God.

Your reason for not forgiving yourself may be linked to any number of different circumstances in your life. It may be because of something that was done to you, where you were helpless in that situation. Although you were not to blame, you may feel a sense of self-loathing. You probably have also made yourself feel guilty for the offence, instead of realising and accepting that you had nothing to do with it. Nothing destroys one's value and self-esteem more than the depressing recall of the hurts relating to the past. All this is what makes you the hardest person for you to forgive.

Apply God's mercy to yourself

God wants you to be free of the pain, the suffering and the repeated cycle of negative feelings towards yourself and others. From the day you were born again and made a child of God, the freedom Christ paid for through His shed blood became yours.

None of us deserve anything from God. When you come to Him for forgiveness and for mercy, it cannot be on the basis of anything you have done as if you deserve it. Anything done that suggests you deserve His mercy is a dead work, an exercise in self-righteousness. His forgiveness and mercy is because of everything He has done. Everything that He has made available to you comes from His grace and is received by faith. When you begin to understand such forgiveness and mercy, the first person you need to apply it to is yourself. Once you receive God's mercy to forgive yourself, you can then be merciful and forgive others.

After I was born again, I was so filled with the love of God I just wanted to forgive everyone. But suddenly reality hit me. I realised that I kept making the same mistakes, falling and failing repeatedly. I questioned God about it. He said the reason that I perpetuated the pain of the failures of my past was because I had not forgiven myself.

We have already seen that the Word tells us to love God with all our heart and to love our neighbour as ourselves. *(Matthew 22:37-39.)* So when we truly love God, we receive His mercy, and the first person we need to pour that mercy upon is ourselves. If we do not pour it on ourselves, we will have nothing to give others. I may want to run around and forgive the whole world, but while the most significant person in my life after God remains unforgiven by me, my efforts at forgiving others will be empty, and I will find myself tripping over the same old problems because I remain attached to them.

You may be experiencing inner turmoil. Perhaps you are struggling because you despise the culture or the family you grew up in. You might resent the name you were given or the gender you were created. Perhaps you regret living in the country where you are or your country of origin. You may also regret the education you received. All this means you are trapped in the pain of your past and you have nothing to give your neighbour. You do not value who you are in God. You are not living as a child of God should by letting the Holy Spirit lead you. And your regrets have become hurts that you are holding on to instead of receiving God's mercy and forgiving yourself so you can be released to bring God's mercy to others.

Receive God's mercy now, and forgive yourself for holding on to your hurt and pain. Thank God for what He has done for you. Repent and receive His forgiveness and rejoice in the blessing of His mercy by letting go of the things that have troubled you. Then enjoy loving others as God has loved you.

Choose not to remember the past

The next important principle to apply in order to love yourself and to walk in the freedom of forgiveness is this: when you repent of your sin and receive His forgiveness, do as God does and choose not to remember the past. It is a wonderful thing that *if we confess our sins, He is faithful and just to forgive us our sins and to cleanse us from all unrighteousness. 1 John 1:9.* But what is also truly wonderful is that God chooses not to remember our sins. *"I, even I, am He who blots out your transgressions for My own sake; And I will not remember your sins." Isaiah 43:25.*

After you have received God's mercy and forgiven yourself, you must choose not to think about all the situations which have been released through God's forgiveness. Now you have forgiven yourself, there's nothing to hold on to. Once you have forgiven others, they and you have been released. So, let go of the past. With God's help, choose not to remember. Forget the past.

But the devil will continually try to remind you of the hurts relating to the past. This keeps you in captivity to your past and a sense of condemnation continues to live in you. *There is therefore now no condemnation to those who are in Christ Jesus, who do not walk according to the flesh, but according to the Spirit. For the law of the Spirit of life in Christ Jesus has made me free from the law of sin and death. Romans 8:1-2.* What a tragedy to live life as if you are still subject to the law of sin and death!

Forgetting may seem difficult, but there is something you can do which will help you; reach forward to those things which are ahead. Follow the apostle Paul's wise counsel: *One thing I do, forgetting those things which are behind and reaching forward to those things which are ahead, I press toward the goal for the prize of the upward call of God in Christ Jesus. Philippians 3:13-14.* Stop living in the past and start living in the present. Focus on God's purpose for your life and get on with what He has called you to do. Join with others in building church and become an effective part of it. That is the primary thing God has called you to. It is from that base He will reveal what else He has for you and your hurtful memories will fade because of the joy of moving forward.

Learn from your past and move on

Here's an illustration to help you learn from your past and move on. There was a large fruit tree that blew over in a storm. When the farmer was asked what he was going to do about it he explained, "There's fruit on the branches. I'm going to gather the fruit. Then I'm going to burn the tree, plant a new tree and move on." And that is exactly what he did. He gathered the fruit, planted a new tree and moved on.

The key is to learn from our past and move on. Yes, we need to pick the fruit, but we also need to move on. Notice that the farmer burned the tree. We need to take all those things that have kept us imprisoned, those past wounds, bruises, hurts and mistakes, put them on God's altar and burn them.

Speak to your past situations, declaring to them, "You no longer exist. The hurts of my past no longer define who I am. I am not defined as a person by the colour of my skin, my culture, the country I come from, my gender or my education (or whatever else it was). God defines me, for I am a spirit and I was born upon this earth to be significant, to fulfil my God-ordained destiny, to leave a history of God's grace and mercy in and through my life."

Do not camp at the burned down tree

Learn from each painful situation. Take from it what you can and burn the rest. But too many of us camp at the burned down tree, remembering 'the good old days' despite the challenges and difficulties they brought to our lives. Were they so good?

People quickly forget that not so very long ago there was no television and the radio kept crackling. Now I have digital, which gives me pure sound. Computers did not exist back then. Today I have a personal computer. If there had been a computer in the fifties, it would have taken up the space of about three blocks on a housing estate just for the machinery. I now put my computer in my bag and I can walk around with it. And what about communication systems? If you are old enough to remember the early dial telephones, you will remember that the reception was really bad and, in some cases, neighbours could listen in on your call.

You were younger, more ignorant, you did not know all you know now and you lived with the hang-ups of the people around you. Not everything was good in those days, but when we 'camp at the burned down tree', all we can see is what used to be and we live trapped in distorted memories, as well as hurts of the past.

God has provided for all your needs

God has done everything you need to live a full and free life as He had always planned and purposed for you. He has left nothing undone and His Word is the source of His provision for you. By His Spirit dwelling in you, He makes it possible for you to love like Him. It is Christ in you that makes such love, mercy and forgiveness possible. Peter put it this way: *Grace and peace be multiplied to you in the knowledge of God and of Jesus our Lord, as His divine power has given to us all things that pertain to life and godliness, through the knowledge of Him who called us by glory and virtue, by which have been given to us exceedingly great and precious promises, that through these you may be partakers of the divine nature, having escaped the corruption that is in the world through lust. 2 Peter 1:2-4.*

In order to forgive yourself and enter into all that God has purposed for you, pray this prayer with all sincerity in your heart:

"Heavenly Father, I thank you for the work of the cross, that Jesus shed His blood and paid the price for my sin. I ask you to forgive me for not walking in the freedom which you purchased for me and for living in condemnation because of how I have seen my past. On the basis of your Word, I declare that all my sins have been washed away, that you have put your nature in me and I am your child.

"I praise you that your love, mercy and grace in my life have made me free and I choose to forgive myself and allow you to live in me and love others through me. Thank you that your Word says that I have been fearfully and wonderfully made. I will respect and rejoice in who you have created me to be. I will esteem myself as valuable in your sight. I acknowledge and declare that from this moment, the enemy no longer has authority over my life because today the chains have been broken.

"Thank You Lord that you have forgotten all my sins and my past. Now I choose to forget what has been forgiven. I will not bring them to my remembrance again to hold on to them. I thank you for your healing and restoration and I move forward according to your will and your Word. Thank you Lord that you continue to perfect the work that you have started in me. In the name of Jesus. Amen."

Forgive yourself by applying God's mercy to your life. Learn from the past and move on to experience all that God has for you as you let His love and counsel be ever present in your life each day. By faith focus on His purpose for your life and enjoy your freedom.

PART FOUR
JESUS AND FORGIVENESS

CHAPTER NINE

LIVING AND FORGIVING WITH JESUS

Life is a journey which becomes increasingly more interesting as we live it with Jesus. Sometimes it can be painful because we all fall short of His example, particularly concerning forgiveness. For this reason God has made provision for us to push beyond our own limitations into the limitlessness of our heavenly Father. He has provided us all with a pattern and plan which is revealed through His Son.

Before we look at the place of forgiveness in Jesus' life, we must first be certain that His example is without fault and is therefore one to which we should aspire. If we are not convinced of that, we've got a long way to go. In considering the lifestyle of Jesus, we observe important principles which form the foundation of a forgiving character.

Jesus condemned behaviour, not people

Jesus' whole nature and everything He did was shaped by and reflected the same heart of love as His Father. This is how He was able to love the sinner, although He never agreed with the sin. Jesus did not come to earth to bring condemnation to mankind. He came to bring a standard of life that we could attain with His help. The Bible tells us: *"God did not send His Son into the world to condemn the world, but that the world through Him might be saved." John 3:17.*

The wonderful thing is that whenever God asks us to do anything, He does not expect us to achieve it in our own strength and abilities. He puts His power, His nature and His character in us, which enables us to live as He does, motivated by a heart of compassion. It is this that makes forgiveness possible.

Jesus replaced legalism by life in the Spirit

Jesus frequently condemned the legalistic attitudes and lifestyles of the scribes and Pharisees, the religious leaders of His time. But we need to note that most of us are prone to imposing our standards on others with almost cold detachment. We even persuade ourselves that we are doing it for the other person's wellbeing, when in fact it's more about our self-righteousness than their 'good'.

Jesus explained to His disciples the difference between merely following the letter of the Law and walking in God's righteousness; and to many people it must have been a shock, as it is to people these days, who think grace has little or nothing to do with God's Law. Jesus said: "*Do not think that I came to destroy the Law or the Prophets. I did not come to destroy but to fulfill.*" *Matthew 5:17.* Then in the rest of the chapter Jesus explained how we should live and spoke of a standard higher than mere legalistic rules. The chapter ends with this: "*Therefore you shall be perfect, just as your Father in heaven is perfect.*" *Matthew 5:48.*

It is not then for us to strive to be 'perfect'. Perfectionists can be some of the most intolerable people around, no less so in the church. But this is still God's Word. Therefore it should be abundantly clear that we cannot live this way without God's help, without Him dwelling in us and the Spirit of Truth leading us. In this way, *I can do all things through Christ who strengthens me,* as Paul wrote to the *Philippians (4:13).* The life God wants us to live becomes possible when we get hold of the truth of Jesus' words: "*With men this is impossible, but with God all things are possible.*" *Matthew 19:26.* Then we submit to His will, ways and Word so it does become possible.

Jesus' devotion to the Father directed His life

It might seem an odd statement to make, but even today some people want to imitate what they believe Jesus would have looked like, growing long hair and a beard. That's just an empty show. What we should imitate about Christ is not the style of His dress, but the manner of His life.

The ruling principle in the life of Jesus was His love for the Father. Everything began there; that was His foundation. We can only follow His example if we too have an abiding love for God the Father, because Jesus said, *"I and My Father are one." John 10:30.* And He also said, *"He who has seen Me, has seen the Father...." John 14:9.*

Jesus knew He could do nothing without the Father. Often He would spend all night alone with Him away from the crowds and even away from His own disciples. Even after performing amazing miracles, which we might consider to be some of the greatest moments of His life, He would disappear to be with His Father again.

If only we followed Jesus' example! Our intimate devotion to God is too easily sidelined because we allow our natural instincts to determine our response to Him. We even allow our interaction with others to interfere as if more important and preferable. For example, after achieving any sort of success, or if God performs a miracle through us, we want recognition and attention from others. We quickly forget that it was God who enabled us. Our first response is rarely to leave the crowd in order to thank Him and be with Him. Instead, we stay among our audience, waiting for someone to give us praise and admiration and tell us what a great, godly person we are. Often our response is apparently humble, "Not me, but Him," while in our hearts we are thinking, "I'm glad you noticed." We don't give God the credit or the glory. We take it ourselves, because of our pride.

This is why we too need to know, believe and act in the certainty that we can do nothing without the Father. Our relationship and our communion with Him should be as intimate and devoted as that of His Son.

Jesus' obedience to the Father's will flowed from this devotion

When we love the Father and we are devoted to Him, obedience to Him will never be a burdensome duty. It will just be a matter of flowing with Him as we obey His Word and His will in every area of life. Forgiveness will become a natural part of our lifestyle, an expression of a heart motivated by love.

Although Jesus was in society, He did not succumb to its temptations as He sought to seek and save the lost. Jesus was misunderstood, persecuted and hated by the very people He came to save, but it did not harden His heart or cause Him to walk away from His responsibilities. The same cannot be said of so many of us. Many of us walk away from our responsibilities and even hesitate to forgive. When we are misunderstood, persecuted or hated, forgiveness is the last thing on our minds. When we do something to help others, even if it is only simple, and they respond negatively, our attitudes towards them are far from the way Jesus would have responded. We must take to heart the words of Jesus: *"I am the vine, you are the branches. He who abides in Me, and I in him, bears much fruit; for without Me you can do nothing." John 15:5.*

Jesus forgave people even though they did not ask Him to

The Bible recounts many occasions when Jesus forgave people. He frequently told people that their sins were forgiven. Interestingly, people did not come to Him and ask Him to forgive their sins; Jesus forgave them without being asked. We need to follow His example in this. Even in the midst of being persecuted, Jesus was already forgiving His persecutors.

Can you forgive someone while they are still in the process of hurting you? What most of us do first is become angry or indignant and go through a whole range of other emotions. We tell ourselves that the other person's behaviour was totally unjustified. Who do they think they are? Then, perhaps, we imagine what we would like to do to them if we weren't Christians.

Then the light of God's love and mercy pours into us. We are reminded that He should have put us to death because of our sin, but He didn't. And we cry out, ashamed, "Oh, yes, forgive me Lord!" You may have already experienced this, and there will probably be times when you will experience it again. But if you remember God's love and mercy for you, you will forgive people even though they do not ask you to.

Jesus sought forgiveness from God for others

We all need God's help continually, because we all fall short of His glory and standards. Even though we may do the right thing by asking for God's forgiveness for judging others, and even though we may release them to Him, the righteous Judge, Jesus wants to take us a step further still.

Once again, it is Jesus who sets the example. He never gave any indication that He believed other people's behaviour towards Him was unjust, unfair or offensive. He was beaten, spat upon, insulted, mocked and rejected. Because of who He was, He had every just reason for complaining about what they did. He was so meek; powerful but restrained in the interests of those He came to save. When Jesus was surrounded and about to be taken away, His disciples were prepared to fight, but Jesus said to them: *Do you think that I cannot now pray to My Father, and He will provide Me with more than twelve legions of angels? Matthew 26:53*. Then He let the soldiers take Him to His torture and death. Here we see a graphic example of the meekness of compassion with a heart to forgive.

Later on, while hanging on the cross experiencing the worst torture and punishment man could put Him through, He did not forget what the Father had called Him to do for you and me. Instead,

Jesus sought forgiveness from the Father for His persecutors: *"Father, forgive them, for they do not know what they do." Luke 23:34.*

Jesus always pleads with God on our behalf. Even though the Word tells us that judgment is coming, Jesus still intercedes for us, asking His Father not to bring that judgment on us or put it to our account. As the Bible says: *Therefore He is also able to save to the uttermost those who come to God through Him, since He always lives to make intercession for them. Hebrews 7:25.*

We too should position ourselves as intercessors for all who mistreat us, but often our heart attitude lets us down. We may believe we have forgiven and released them, but inwardly think something like, "Thank God they're off my back. Now I hope they suffer. They deserve it." We want God to sort them out and some people may even want God to strike dead those who have hurt them. We believe we have a right to think this way. Even though we release people, our attitude causes us to feel a certain sense of smugness and satisfaction when we hear that things have gone wrong for them. We may say, "What a shame...", but think, "What do you expect..." God is not mocked; He sees and will judge our hearts for our hypocrisy. We forget we should all be dead but for God's grace.

Positioning ourselves as intercessor for those who have hurt us requires us to rise above our human frailty and natural inclinations. That takes forgiveness to a new level. Note what Jesus said to His Father after pleading with Him to forgive His persecutors; He asked Him to forgive them, adding, *"For they do not know what they do." Luke 23-34.* The issue of the other person's sin is for God to deal with, but because it is something that affects us, we must forgive and release them to God.

In reality, we may well suffer as a result of someone else's actions or words. But look to Jesus. Who has suffered more than He did as the result of what other people so unjustly did and said? No sin was found in Him, no unforgiveness. *"Father forgive them..."*

Jesus loved Judas

Consider Judas' betrayal of Jesus and our Lord's attitude towards him. There is controversy among believers and theologians concerning whether Judas' action was held to his account and whether he will be in heaven. When we arrive there, we may be surprised to see people we never thought would make it, but it is not our place to judge; just be absolutely sure that you do not miss heaven yourself.

It was before the Feast of the Passover, and Jesus knew that His time on earth was drawing to a close. *John 13:1* states that He would soon *depart from this world to the Father, having loved His own who were in the world, He loved them to the end.* Bible commentaries generally agree that His own refers to the twelve disciples and all those in the world who would believe in Him until the end of time. *To the end* suggests both the limitlessness of Jesus' love, as well as its intensity. Judas was included as one of *His own who were in the world*, whom He loved to the end.

Jesus treated Judas and the other disciples in the same way

Even though the devil had already put it into the heart of Judas to betray Jesus, and even though Jesus knew what was going to happen, He still washed the feet of Judas along with the other disciples. Jesus explained through what He did that the humility and devotion of a servant should be a characteristic of all His disciples: *"If I then, your Lord and Teacher, have washed your feet, you also ought to wash one another's feet. For I have given you an example, that you should do as I have done to you." John 13:14-15.* Jesus didn't turn to Judas and say: "I know what you're up to," and pass by on the other side. Jesus showed the same humility and love to Judas as He did to the other disciples. He exhorts us to do likewise, even to those who would betray us.

Later at the supper table the story of Jesus' betrayal by Judas continued to unfold: *"Most assuredly, I say to you, one of you will betray Me." Then the disciples looked at one another, perplexed about whom He spoke. Now there was leaning on Jesus' bosom one of His disciples, whom Jesus loved. Simon Peter therefore motioned to Him to ask who it was of whom He spoke. Then, leaning back on Jesus' breast, he said to Him, "Lord, who is it?" Jesus answered, "It is he to whom I shall give a piece of bread when I have dipped it." John 13:21-26.*

We are not told whether the other disciples heard Jesus' reply to Simon Peter. However, what is said next illustrates that they did not know that it was Judas who was about to betray Jesus: *And having dipped the bread, He gave it to Judas Iscariot, the son of Simon. Now after the piece of bread, Satan entered him. Then Jesus said to him, "What you do, do quickly." But no-one at the table knew for what reason He said this to him. John 13:26-28.* Possibly Judas himself did not even know what Jesus had said to Simon Peter. Anyway, Judas took the bread, Satan entered him and then he left the others.

Jesus prayed for ALL His disciples

From chapter 13 to the end of chapter 16 in John's gospel, we find Jesus speaking to the disciples. He was teaching and explaining godly principles, with His mind very much on the future and what they would need without His physical presence with them. The content of chapter 17 was still in the same discourse and still in the same timeframe. In this chapter we read of the love, devotion and reverence Jesus had for His Father. After seeking the Father's help for Himself, He turned His attention to pray for His disciples: *"Now I am no longer in the world, but these are in the world, and I did come to You. Holy Father, keep through Your name those whom You have given Me, that they may be one as We are." John 17:11.*

Jesus' heartfelt prayer was for **all** the disciples. I believe this included Judas. Jesus was about to go to the cross and hang there. He was telling His Father that He had faithfully kept them while He was on earth, but that now He was departing He would be depending on the Father to keep them. Jesus prayed for Him to preserve, sustain and support them; He prayed for their unity and that their relationship with one another would be as closely knit as His with the Father.

Jesus continued: *"While I was with them in the world, I kept them in Your name. Those whom You gave Me I have kept; and none of them is lost except the son of perdition, that the Scripture might be fulfilled." John 17:12.* Before the beginning of time, the Father knew what Judas was going to do. When Judas betrayed Jesus, scripture was fulfilled, but I believe it didn't end there.

Jesus continued to pray for all the disciples: *"But now I come to You, and these things I speak in the world, that they may have My joy fulfilled in themselves. I have given them Your word; and the world has hated them because they are not of the world, just I am not of the world. I do not pray that You should take them out of the world, but that You should keep them from the evil one." John 17:13-15.* This time Jesus asked the Father to keep His disciples, and specifically protect them from the devil. His prayer did not exclude Judas or any of His disciples as He focused on the future. His prayer still included the one who would betray Him. His heart of forgiveness knew no limit.

Jesus prayed for ALL His disciples to be sanctified

Then Jesus prayed: *"They are not of the world, just as I am not of the world. Sanctify them by Your truth. Your word is truth. As You sent Me into the world, I also have sent them into the world. And for their sakes I sanctify Myself, that they also may be sanctified by the truth." John 17:16-19.* Jesus asked His Father to sanctify - to dedicate, set apart, make holy - all His disciples. This sanctification is a spiritual work that only comes through God as He applies His Word to our lives. Should Judas have repented, there still was a place for Him. When we understand the closeness of Jesus' relationship with the Father, it's not difficult to believe that Jesus still included Judas in His prayers, that he be kept and sanctified.

Jesus demonstrated utter selflessness in seeking forgiveness for others. His selflessness positioned and empowered Him to endure everything in order for people to be sanctified and for Him to be resurrected to give us eternal life. This is important for us today. If we fail to pray for those who do evil to us and despitefully use us, we will obstruct God's work in our lives and be less that what God purposed for us.

Judas was not present at Jesus' resurrection but I believe we should never assume that he will not be present in eternity. Jesus loved him, prayed for him until the end and held nothing to his account. Regardless of what others do to us, it is not our place to judge but to reach out continually to everyone, just as Jesus demonstrated in his relationship with Judas, His betrayers and His persecutors.

Let Jesus' attitude towards Judas humble and inspire you to love, serve and treat others with compassion. Bring the light of God's Word into every situation. Forgive those who misuse you and intercede for them and ask God to help, keep and sanctify them. Follow Jesus by letting His nature fill you so He can empower you to live a life of compassion and forgiveness. Let His character, nature and power within you be the life from which forgiveness flows.

CHAPTER TEN

FORGIVE AND BE FORGIVEN

Jesus doesn't just leave us to fend for ourselves in life. Concerning forgiveness, even after teaching us and demonstrating the 'how to', He continues to reach out to us, communicating through His relationship with us as individuals. His Word constantly exhorts us to implement what He has revealed and His Spirit is within us to help us follow through and obey the Word.

Ask others for forgiveness

As important as it is for us to forgive others, we also need forgiveness from those we have offended, hurt or harmed. Jesus Himself warned us not to leave any stone unturned in obtaining that forgiveness.

Many people think that because we are now under God's grace and no longer under Law that we do not have to be overly concerned about how we live, "After all," they say, "God is a God of grace. He loves and forgives." As they stand, these statements are true, but not the whole truth.

We no longer need a sacrificial system and its laws to draw near to God, that's true. There has been one sacrifice for sin which is effective for all time, and that was what Jesus became as He hung on the cross. But God's standards of life and living have not changed. In fact, because now we have the benefit of the indwelling Holy Spirit,

He now says: *Therefore you shall be perfect, just as your Father in heaven is perfect. Matthew 5:48.* He now addresses us on the basis of His life in us. Paul expresses this wonderful truth in his letter to the Colossians: *To them God willed to make known what are the riches of the glory of this mystery among the Gentiles: which is Christ in you, the hope of glory. Colossians 1:27.*

It is true that the *law of the Spirit of life in Christ Jesus has made me free from the law of sin and death. Romans 8:2.* But consider the breadth of purpose that lies within the grace of God. *For the grace of God that brings salvation has appeared to all men, teaching us that, denying ungodliness and worldly lusts, we should live soberly, righteously, and godly in the present age, looking for the blessed hope and glorious appearing of our great God and Savior Jesus Christ, who gave Himself for us, that He might redeem us from every lawless deed and purify for Himself His own special people, zealous for good works. Titus 2:11-14.*

So we shouldn't be surprised at how challenging Jesus became when He spoke to His followers as he brought teaching to align people with God's Word and His kingdom: *"You have heard that it was said to those of old, 'You shall not murder, and whoever murders will be in danger of the judgment. But I say to you that whoever is angry with his brother without a cause shall be in danger of the judgment. And whoever says to his brother, 'Raca!' shall be in danger of the council. But whoever says, 'You fool!' shall be in danger of hell fire." Matthew 5:21-22.*

This is one of several comparisons Jesus made between the old and the new law, or the natural and the spiritual law. The 'council', or any other earthly law court, merely punishes outward actions. The thoughts and intents of the heart, which are the root cause of these actions, are to be our primary concern. Jesus therefore exhorts us to go beyond the natural law in order to fulfil God's higher spiritual purpose. This is the only way to avoid eternal punishment and hell fire, as He put it. This is a warning to deal with sin in whatever shape or form it appears, and particularly in the area of how we relate to others.

Jesus gives us the opportunity to put things right

Jesus instructs us to put things right with other people as a priority: *"Therefore if you bring your gift to the altar, and there remember that your brother has something against you, leave your gift there before the altar, and go your way. First be reconciled to your brother, and then come and offer your gift. Agree with your adversary quickly, while you are on the way with him, lest your adversary deliver you to the judge, the judge hand you over to the officer, and you be thrown into prison. Assuredly, I say to you, you will by no means get out of there till you have paid the last penny." Matthew 5: 23-26.* Our Christian faith is seriously undermined if we don't seek forgiveness where we've wronged someone.

If the Holy Spirit brings to your remembrance that your brother has something against you, it is because of something that you have done or said. He doesn't make it up and He doesn't bring it to mind for you to think about it and ponder the rights and wrongs. He expects you to get on with it and seek the other person's forgiveness.

It's also worth noting that the Holy Spirit will not remind you of what others have done to you. If something does come to mind, it is almost always because of your inclination to justify yourself or wallow in your hurts. Let it go, put it down. If you hang on to it, the hurt will become a bruise, and we've already spoken about what happens then.

Do whatever it takes to obtain the forgiveness of others

If you know you have wronged someone and you do not go and seek their forgiveness and be reconciled to them, you are in trouble. Do everything you possibly can to obtain the forgiveness of others, even if it is going to be painful.

When I was in business in South Africa, some people I employed and trusted acted inappropriately. What they did put my company in a very serious financial situation which I had absolutely no way of salvaging. All I could do was to go to the person we owed the most money and to apologise and seek his forgiveness. My words were not met with grace. I sat there opposite him and his anger exploded as he used every expletive imaginable. If he had never taken much notice before of the fact that I was a Christian and a minister, he certainly referred to it now, letting me know what he thought of me as a Christian in no uncertain terms.

I wanted to defend myself against his onslaught. I wanted to point out that it wasn't really my fault; but the Holy Spirit had other ideas. The Holy Spirit told me to sit down and shut up. The Spirit spoke to me and explained that what had happened was because of the mistakes that I had made. He said that my employees had put me in this situation because I had not properly controlled or managed them and that I must release my employees from any responsibility. The Holy Spirit concluded by adding that I should let that man say what he had to say and not justify myself.

I obeyed the Holy Spirit. I sat down and shut up. When my creditor had eventually finished, I left his office. I felt lower than I ever had before, but I knew I had followed the instruction of the Holy Spirit.

Three months later, the Holy Spirit prompted me to go and see this man again and to make my financial situation clear. During our meeting, I told him truthfully, "I just want you to know I'll do whatever it takes, but I can't repay you." He said to me just this one thing: "What do you want out of this - your car, your house - what is it you want?" I replied, "I don't want anything. I just want my name. That's all I have."

Then something amazing happened which I could never have anticipated. He turned round and called his wife, who was the Company Secretary, and said to her, "I'm wiping this man's debt out completely." With that, he turned back to me, saying, "That's it. You don't owe me a penny."

It did not even end there. I also owed another creditor a great deal of money. The man phoned him and instructed him to wipe out everything that I owed him too. As I heard what was said, I was astonished and speechless.

I could never have foreseen what had now been achieved. Through seeking forgiveness when I knew I had done wrong, and releasing those who had wronged me, I experienced the power of forgiveness through the very person I had wronged. That same man to whom I owed so much had become my deliverer.

Relationships are more important to God than reason

Our natural inclination when we are in the wrong is to hide. Then, when things become really serious, we send for a lawyer to defend us because it is always easier when somebody else represents us. But there are times, as I experienced, when God tells us that we must go in person. It is not easy to obey when we do not want to admit that we are wrong, because pride gets in the way. Pride is still what controls Satan today and it is the only thing that will stop you from asking for forgiveness.

We have already seen in *Matthew 5:24* that God wants us to seek reconciliation. This applies even if something is not our fault, because reconciliation is not an option. It is the calling of our ministry. It is more important to God that we are reconciled in our relationships with others than it is for us to be right. We are usually very good at justifying ourselves and giving reasons for our wrong behaviour, but God always places greater emphasis on relationships than reason.

I could have denied the truth of my failings and hired a lawyer to defend me even though I was wrong. I might have refused to swallow my pride to ask personally for forgiveness. I could have ignored the fact that Jesus tells us to ask others for forgiveness and that He provides opportunities to put things right. I could have overlooked the fact that I should do whatever it takes to obtain forgiveness from others. I did not initially understand that my relationship with this man was important to God.

If I had not heeded Jesus' instructions and the prompting of the Holy Spirit, I would never have learned the power of forgiveness. I am sure my life would have taken a very different course. I would most certainly not have experienced the joy, victory and fulfilment which have been my experience since. I have no doubt I would not be where I am today, spiritually and in every other respect. Through this one man's forgiveness, the debt incurred because of my past mistakes concerning the business were wiped clean and I was given a new start. This is so much like what happens when we come to Jesus and our sins are forgiven. Our debt is wiped clean and we are given a new start.

Blessing is the result of forgiving and being forgiven

In considering life with Jesus as our example, we have looked at some of the things that He taught and said on the subject. We have seen how He demonstrated forgiveness in His own life, and recognised that He instructed us to forgive and seek forgiveness without hesitation. In all of this, there are indisputable benefits to ourselves and to others when we live in forgiveness. There is a particular promise that Jesus made concerning forgiveness that illustrates God's loving and generous heart towards us. He promised that blessing follows forgiveness.

I have not only discovered this for myself through my own experiences, but I have seen it demonstrated time and time again in the lives of others. The promise of receiving God's blessing here on earth as well as in heaven is surely one of the greatest promises God has given us. It is fulfilled when we heed His instruction and warnings, and obey Him. Jesus tells us in *Matthew 5:7, "Blessed are the merciful, for they shall obtain mercy."* The Amplified Bible reads: *"Blessed (happy, to be envied, and spiritually prosperous ---- with life-joy and satisfaction in God's favour and salvation, regardless of their outward conditions) are the merciful, for they shall obtain mercy!*

Nothing can compare to the limitless way in which God wants to bless us if we will forgive and be forgiven. Let's not forfeit God's blessings!

Don't be tempted to enjoy a moment of smug self-satisfaction at holding on to what you think is your right not to forgive, or to take brief pleasure at seeing those who have hurt you suffer. None of these temporal, fleshly emotions can even begin to scratch the surface of the blessedness and the blessings that God will place in your life, if you will let go of the temporal and pursue the eternal.

There's nothing quite like waking up each morning with joy in your heart and praise on your lips because your conscience is clear before God. As *Psalm 30:5* says: *His anger is but for a moment, His favor is for life; Weeping may endure for a night, but joy comes in the morning.* And in his letter to the Romans, Paul writes: *David also describes the blessedness of the man to whom God imputes righteousness apart from works: "BLESSED ARE THOSE WHOSE LAWLESS DEEDS ARE FORGIVEN, AND WHOSE SINS ARE COVERED; BLESSED IS THE MAN TO WHOM THE LORD SHALL NOT IMPUTE SIN." Romans 4:6-8.*

Note that if we do not forgive or seek forgiveness, we sin, and it is imputed to us and we lose the blessings of God. But in doing what is right before God, you will walk free and experience the joy in your heart that is the result of God's grace, mercy and abundant blessings.

We all need the presence of God in our lives because without it, there is no future, no eternity and no hope. There is no-one so squeaky clean that they do not need to repent. It is God's love that exposes our sin and gives us opportunity to receive His forgiveness.

If your heart is troubled because you know there is an issue which requires forgiveness, either it concerns you forgiving another or you needing forgiveness, I invite you to say this prayer with all sincerity:

"Father, I thank you for your love and mercy which you pour so abundantly into my life. I realise I am already forgiven because of what Jesus did at Calvary when He died for me. But you expect me to come and ask for your forgiveness, and then to release those who have mistreated or harmed me and seek out those who have something against me. Thank you Lord that because you love me, you correct me.

"I recognise that I have sinned against you. Be merciful to me, a sinner; cleanse me from unrighteousness, from my hardened heart, my stubbornness and my pride. Grant me your mercy and forgive me. Thank you for revealing and demonstrating to me the beauty of your nature and your love through my Lord and Saviour, Jesus Christ. Thank you that your grace helps me to live in accordance with your Word so that I can enjoy the freedom that was bought with the blood of Christ.

"I honour, love and worship you Father. In the name of Jesus. Amen."

Be determined to live a lifestyle of forgiveness. Grasp the opportunities Jesus gives you to put things right when you miss the mark. Do whatever is necessary to deepen your relationship with Him. Always rejoice in the knowledge that you are forgiven. Open your heart to receive the blessings God pours out to those who live the life of forgiveness. Live in the freedom of forgiveness!

CONCLUSION

FORGIVENESS, THE KEY TO FREEDOM

As a pastor and leader in the international Christian community I have had to help people, time and time again, deal with the causes and consequences of unforgiveness. It can be quite distressing to see the destructiveness of unforgiveness in their lives. Out of this I felt compelled by the Holy Spirit to share my experience and understanding of the subject of forgiveness in this book.

To benefit from this book requires an open and honest heart from the reader. God cares deeply about you and desires that you enjoy the freedom He has prepared for you through the shed blood of our Lord Jesus Christ. If in any respect you realise that because of unforgiveness you are included in what is written in this book, I strongly encourage you to take time to work through the principles set out here and follow through on the process that will lead to your freedom.

Expect God to change your life as you apply His principles. Be made free and continue to walk free, doing all that you can with God's help to remain in that place of freedom.

I encourage you to remind yourself continually of Paul's exhortation to the Galatians: *Stand fast therefore in the liberty by which Christ has made us free, and do not be entangled again with a yoke of bondage. Galatians 5:1.*

An important part of loving your neighbour as yourself *(Romans 13:9-10)* is to take care of your spiritual health at least as much if not more that you take care of your physical health. Your spiritual heart needs your attention. I encourage you to examine yourself continually in the light of the Word of God to make sure your relationship with your heavenly Father is full and free. At any sign of unforgiveness, run to Him for healing. *If we confess our sins, He is faithful and just to forgive us our sins and to cleanse us from all unrighteousness. 1 John 1:9.*

The Holy Spirit is your Helper. As you listen to the Holy Spirit and follow His promptings, your life will become aligned with God's Word and your relationship with the Father will grow. Then the wonderful thing is that the more His life fills out your life, the less likely it will be that you will ever hold on to someone in unforgiveness.

I cannot promise that life's circumstances will never again cause you to experience hurt or pain. But I can promise you that you will now be equipped to receive forgiveness, to forgive others and yourself and to walk in forgiveness, the key to freedom.

REV GERRI DI SOMMA

COMING OUT OF THE DARKNESS
Faith Steps to Receiving from God

When, through circumstances, darkness descends even on the believer, this book offers godly, life-changing principles and lasting solutions. It draws from the miracle of Bartimaeus and his meeting with Jesus, guiding and teaching the young believer and challenging the mature to new heights. Questions at the end of each chapter help individual or group study, encouraging all to come out of their darkness into the light of their own miracle.

LIVING FREE
From Deception

This is essential reading because deception affects everyone at some time. It destroys faith, damages relationships with God and others, thwarting God's plans and purposes on earth and for eternity. This inspired teaching and godly wisdom help identify and redress belief in falsehood and disbelief in truth. Questions after each chapter facilitate personal or group study. Spiritual principles and clear illustrations guide and equip the reader to overcome and avoid deception. It points the way for every reader to experience spiritual growth and change as they enjoy life, free from deception.

MEN OF PURPOSE

A mini-book which tackles reasons why men aren't functioning as God designed them, as leaders in their church and community. This book challenges men to overcome obstacles in their own lives to become '**Men of Purpose**'.

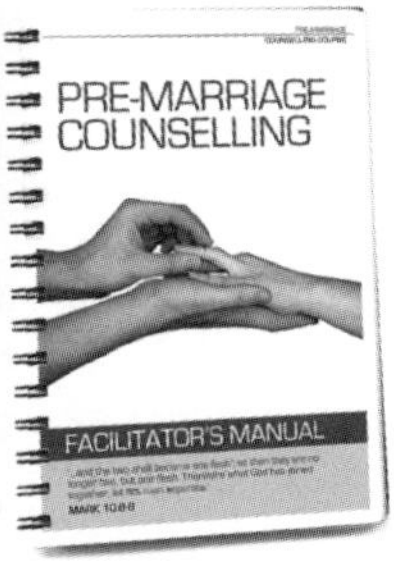

PRE-MARITAL COUNSELLING
Training Manual for Ministers

A comprehensive training course for ministers, trainee ministers, pastors, teachers and others involved in the work of the Gospel. Its aim is to equip them to prepare couples for a happy, successful, life long marriage which follows God's blueprint. It contains clear guidelines based on God's Word and also includes worksheets to be used as facilitating tools.

All publications and an extensive range of other materials are available from Carmel Book Shop. www.carmelbookshop